Good
Orderly
Direction

Ayin M. Adams, Ph.D.

**DELANE
PUBLISHING**

Copyright © Ayin M. Adams, Ph.D. 2014

ISBN-13
978-0-9840204-8-5

ISBN-10
0-9840204-8-9

First Edition: January 3, 2014

Cover Design and Typesetting by Saforabu Graphix

Published by Delane Publishing
P.O. Box 195, Wailuku, Maui, HI 96793 USA
Email: books@delanepublishing.com
www.delanepublishing.com

Published in the United States of America

No part of this book may be reproduced or transmitted in any form or by any means, electronic, photocopying, or otherwise, without the express written consent of the publisher.

Printed in USA

Special Thanks to: Linn Conyers for her spiritual guidance and love.

Books by Ayin M. Adams, Ph.D.

For Ladies Only, Dedicated to the Color Pink

Kwanzaa in Hawai`i

African Americans In Hawai`i: A Search For Identity

The Woods Deep Inside Me

Walking In Sappho's Garden

Walking Through My Fire

Books edited by Ayin M. Adams, Ph.D.

Climbing A Rainbow of Dreams

Butterflies Blossom

From Dawn To Dusk

Graffiti Dreams

Introduction

This book is full of positive daily affirmations and directions for reducing stress and creating inner peace. It is a powerful guide to the reader. Adams offers practical tools for attaining a more compassionate, responsible and fulfilling life and inspires the reader to take charge of his/her problems, relationships, sadness, and life's painful tests and situations. She shows how to redirect energy toward a new inner freedom and more transparent way of being in the world. Adams creates the feeling of a new day and new beginnings.

The themes run from the universal to the personal: the power to see oneself and to change, the rewards of embracing a higher good, and the directions to develop and enhance nurturing relationships. She offers the reader the hope for change through acceptance, spiritual practices, meditations, and moving through inertia and negativity by making right choices. She opens spiritual doors to seeing beyond appearances; she opens the door to Grace.

Ayin Adams is a woman with intention, guided by trust and living in the light of Spirit. She writes as an act of healing, and she speaks with the voice of understanding and compassion. She has lived in a variety of places and situations, on the edge and in the middle of life's blessings and turmoil. She ministers, teaches, heals, counsels, and helps others from all walks of life to gain more control over their emotions, including their fears, and guilt.

Her presence reflects her enthusiasm and contagious energy; her words communicate new ways of understanding and being to help the reader navigate life's ever changing waters and sometimes turbulent situations. She believes in movement and creative waiting, the individual's quest for success on whatever personal path to goodness a person might set. Adams is able to quicken in others and persuade them of their personal abilities to embrace change, channel energy, and accomplish their aims through perseverance and the pursuit of higher principles. She inspires the reader to recognize and reclaim his/her personal power and to see, feel, and walk in a new way.

Her words inspire, just as she herself receives inspiration from Nature's infinite beauty, processes, and changes. She knows that a key to wholeness and fulfillment is about living in the consciousness of now, knowing, loving and healing the Divine self, both physically and spiritually. She understands the necessity of stillness, listening, observing, and patience, in order to find personal inner freedom and a healthy balance between being and doing. Adams understands that a beneficial relationship with self and others is a path to clarity and harmony. The reader will discover his/her essence and learn how to find balance while eliminating stress. This in turn opens the path to a new level of consciousness, an inner glow of well-being, and a more harmonious life.

Kathryn Waddell Takara, PhD
December 10, 2013

GOOD ORDERLY DIRECTION

JANUARY

White Snowdrop

THE NEW YOU, THE NEW YEAR

Yesterday, today, and tomorrow, I live and move in the one. Whatever I am feeling at any moment, I know that I am never alone. Years may come and go, but it is we who change and grow. I know that this is my year. Happy new me. Happy new you.

I receive. I accept. I embrace.

Reflections:

January 2 — **GOOD ORDERLY DIRECTION**

NEW YEAR

Yesterday, today, and tomorrow, I live and move in the one. Whatever I am feeling at any moment, I know that I am never alone.

> The winter's journey
> teaches me inner yearnings
> that this New Year brings

I receive. I accept. I embrace.

Reflections:

Yesterday, today, and tomorrow, I live and move in the one. Whatever I am feeling at any moment, I know that I am never alone. As I enter into the New Year, I know that it is a good time to ask myself questions, "Where have I been?" As I look back, at my life up until this year, "Where have I been?" "Where am I now" financially, or in relationships, or in my spiritual awareness? Where am I now? Where am I going? What does the future hold for me? What is this year going to portend for my life?

I receive. I accept. I embrace.

Reflections:

WHAT IS TIME?

Yesterday, today, and tomorrow, I live and move in the one. Whatever I am feeling at any moment, I know that I am never alone. My questions continue: what is a year? I have never stopped to think about this question, have you? What is a day? What is a minute? What is a second? What is time? I know that what I call a year is more psychological than it is astronomical. It is a convenient way of keeping track of footprints in the sand, but the winds of change very quickly blow them away, now what is left, only the allness of eternity.

I receive. I accept. I embrace.

Reflections: _____
_____
_____
_____
_____
_____

Yesterday, today, and tomorrow, I live and move in the one. Whatever I am feeling at any moment, I know that I am never alone. I believe that I owe it to myself to take inventory, a personal inventory. There is so much that I take for granted in my life. I know that it is advantageous to get a sense of where I am at in consciousness which will enable me to take steps in adjustments and make the most effective commitments in the year ahead.

I receive. I accept. I embrace.

Reflections:

January 6 — **GOOD ORDERLY DIRECTION**

INFINITE LIFE

Yesterday, today, and tomorrow, I live and move in the one. Whatever I am feeling at any moment, I know that I am never alone. I know that one of the things I tend to overlook often when I look at myself is that I am a growing, changing, individualized expression of infinite life.

I receive. I accept. I embrace.

Reflections:

CHANGE

Yesterday, today, and tomorrow, I live and move in the one. Whatever I am feeling at any moment, I know that I am never alone. I know that life is a changing process of growth and unfoldment. I can change by growing through a metamorphosis. It is good for me at this time of the year to realize that no matter what I have evaluated myself as being, no matter what I have done, the main concern is where am I going? What am I reaching for? What am I aspiring to? This tells me much more about what I am.

I receive. I accept. I embrace.

Reflections:

January 8 — **GOOD ORDERLY DIRECTION**

Yesterday, today, and tomorrow, I live and move in the one. Whatever I am feeling at any moment, I know that I am never alone. I must go deeper than deep. I must get honest with myself and ask the questions, am I happy with what has been continually happening in my life? Do I feel passionate about myself, about what's going on? If not, what is it that I think is going on? These questions help me to receive, to accept, and embrace.

I receive. I accept. I embrace.

Reflections:

Yesterday, today, and tomorrow, I live and move in the one. Whatever I am feeling at any moment, I know that I am never alone. If the directions that I know that I need to make a change and devote myself to making those changes in the New Year, am I moving in that direction that I would like to change?

I receive. I accept. I embrace.

Reflections:

January 10 — **GOOD ORDERLY DIRECTION**

METAMORPHOSIS

Yesterday, today, and tomorrow, I live and move in the one. Whatever I am feeling at any moment, I know that I am never alone. Today I dedicate myself to making those changes so that I may experience something of a metamorphosis. I know that this experience of a metamorphosis is potentially possible to me no matter what it is that I am trying to outgrow.

I receive. I accept. I embrace.

Reflections:

UNHAPPEN THINGS

Yesterday, today, and tomorrow, I live and move in the one. Whatever I am feeling at any moment, I know that I am never alone. I know that I cannot change other people. I know that I am not going to change the employer or the wife, the husband, the children, or the next door neighbor. I know that I cannot change circumstances. I cannot unhappen things that have taken place in my life. I know that the greatest cause of unhappiness is the tendency to try and unhappen the thing that has been experienced. There is no way I can do this. But I know that I can receive, accept and embrace.

I receive. I accept. I embrace.

Reflections:

January 12 — GOOD ORDERLY DIRECTION

Yesterday, today, and tomorrow, I live and move in the one. Whatever I am feeling at any moment, I know that I am never alone. Things that exist now are things that have happened in the past. I know that I cannot do anything about them, but I know that I can change the way I see them, and the way I deal with them. I know that I can change my emotions about them. I can decide that I'm not going to re-sense them which means to resent or to feel bitter about them. I let them go. Situations and experiences in my past cannot find any resolution without my willingness to let go.

I receive. I accept. I embrace.

Reflections:

RESENTMENTS

Yesterday, today, and tomorrow, I live and move in the one. Whatever I am feeling at any moment, I know that I am never alone. I know that when I hold any resentment against a person, place, thing, or institution, it is like being urinated on, I am the only one who feels the hot water running down my leg. Today I let go of any resentment.

I receive. I accept. I embrace.

Reflections:

January 14 — **GOOD ORDERLY DIRECTION**

PAST

Yesterday, today, and tomorrow, I live and move in the one. Whatever I am feeling at any moment, I know that I am never alone. Things in my past cannot find any resolution without my willingness to let go. And if I do not let go, it is because I am permitting it to be. When I let go, I let flow the positive.

I receive. I accept. I embrace.

Reflections:

Yesterday, today, and tomorrow, I live and move in the one. Whatever I am feeling at any moment, I know that I am never alone. I love that affirmation of Walt Whitman, when he says, "Oh while I live to be the ruler of life and not a slave, to meet life as a powerful conqueror and nothing exterior shall ever take command of me." I know that no person, no situation, no movement of time, no relationship, no negative happening, can ever take possession of me. I insist that I am a free and individualized expression. I know that I cannot always control what happens, but I can decide that I am going to take hold of it, by the right end.

I receive. I accept. I embrace.

Reflections:

January 16 — **GOOD ORDERLY DIRECTION**

Yesterday, today, and tomorrow, I live and move in the one. Whatever I am feeling at any moment, I know that I am never alone. I have nothing to fear. Divine justice goes before me and prepares the way. Divine justice is Divine nature. Divine justice is the Divine reality of itself. I recognize this truth.

I receive. I accept. I embrace.

Reflections:

FORMING RELATIONSHIPS

Yesterday, today, and tomorrow, I live and move in the one. Whatever I am feeling at any moment, I know that I am never alone. Attention has always been centered on building a winning personality, the mask of the self, almost to the exclusion of the real person behind the mask and this leads to good actors. The truth is that it hinders our ability to form a fulfilling relationship with another, much less to form a relationship with ourselves.

I receive. I accept. I embrace.

Reflections:

January 18 — **GOOD ORDERLY DIRECTION**

Yesterday, today, and tomorrow, I live and move in the one. Whatever I am feeling at any moment, I know that I am never alone. When one hides behind masks, it may lead to indulging in the fantasy that, "Someday my love will come, someday love will happen to me." I know that love never just happens to anyone, it doesn't work that way. Love is not to be found. It is not a matter of finding the right person but being the right person.

I receive. I accept. I embrace.

Reflections:

January 19

Yesterday, today, and tomorrow, I live and move in the one. Whatever I am feeling at any moment, I know that I am never alone. When he/she is being the right person, he/she will eventually attract the right person, and unless one knows this, he/she will tend to place all kinds of unreal expectations on a relationship even before it happens.

I receive. I accept. I embrace.

Reflections:

January 20 — GOOD ORDERLY DIRECTION

Yesterday, today, and tomorrow, I live and move in the one. Whatever I am feeling at any moment, I know that I am never alone. You may look for a partner who will make you feel good, who will make you happy and fulfilled, someone who will make you feel loved, defined, and supported. And your life will be an expectation that things will be changed when you find that right person. And you hold up this burden to lay on the person you dream of coming into your life, an expectation that no one can meet. Of course, it is an extremely selfish motive for forming a relationship coming out of the emphasis on your own inadequacies as a person.

I receive. I accept. I embrace.

Reflections:

Ayin M. Adams, Ph.D. January 21

Yesterday, today, and tomorrow, I live and move in the one. Whatever I am feeling at any moment, I know that I am never alone. It is essential to get back to basics, I am a fabulous beautiful soul in my transcendent self. This is the root of me, the heart of me. I may not know it, but this is what I am and my basic need is not to be loved, but to love. I want someone with whom I can share a mutual experience of growth with. Two people have good grounds for a relationship when each one celebrates what they do have in life, without creating unrealistic expectations on the other to make up for what they do not have. In other words, what I am not should never be a problem, only what I am.

I receive. I accept. I embrace.

Reflections:
_____
_____
_____
_____
_____

January 22 — GOOD ORDERLY DIRECTION

Yesterday, today, and tomorrow, I live and move in the one. Whatever I am feeling at any moment, I know that I am never alone. It is not acceptable to be in a relationship where I think the other has what I do not. I do not get involved out of insecurity or to feel better about myself under the illusion that I am complete. I do not remain in a loveless relationship to rob and steal from the other. Remaining in this relationship emotionally attached through pain, and when there is nothing left to steal or fight about I move on to another who is different from myself, living together with lustful bodies under the same roof that shelters neither, in the same room/bed, but a world apart.

I receive. I accept. I embrace.

Reflections:

Yesterday, today, and tomorrow, I live and move in the one. Whatever I am feeling at any moment, I know that I am never alone. I know that an authentic relationship starts from the premise of each one looking within seeing no lack in self. When I accept my own completion, I can then extend it by joining with another, whole as I am.

I receive. I accept. I embrace.

Reflections:

January 24 — **GOOD ORDERLY DIRECTION**

Yesterday, today, and tomorrow, I live and move in the one. Whatever I am feeling at any moment, I know that I am never alone. Today I base my loving relationship on frankness, and honesty, my enthusiasm for celebrating the game of life together: to love one another for what we are, not for what we are not, or what we perpetually try to be or expect the other person to be.

I receive. I accept. I embrace.

Reflections:

Ayin M. Adams, Ph.D.   January 25

Yesterday, today, and tomorrow, I live and move in the one. Whatever I am feeling at any moment, I know that I am never alone. No longer do I operate from a deficiency of love because I may not have experienced enough love in my childhood. I fully know, and I envelope the realization that I live at the pure heart and center of universal love. I know that my need is to give way to love, to release something within myself which is already there. This means to love myself and to let Spirit love me and to let Spirit be Spirit in me.

I receive. I accept. I embrace.

Reflections:

January 26 — GOOD ORDERLY DIRECTION

Yesterday, today, and tomorrow, I live and move in the one. Whatever I am feeling at any moment, I know that I am never alone. Hungering for a love experience, while expecting it to come from someone else, is never acceptable. Some people reach out and grab it so it will not get away. This behavior is the main motivation that is at the root of so many things we feel and do. This sometimes could mean being swept up into a relationship confusing love with the feelings of flattery.

I receive. I accept. I embrace.

Reflections: _____
_____
_____
_____
_____
_____

Ayin M. Adams, Ph.D. January 27

Yesterday, today, and tomorrow, I live and move in the one. Whatever I am feeling at any moment, I know that I am never alone. If I am fully established in the consciousness of love, I project love to everyone all the time, not just when they are loving because that's the height of spiritual consciousness. I think we all can agree that most of us live a little below that awareness level.

I receive. I accept. I embrace.

Reflections:

January 28 — **GOOD ORDERLY DIRECTION**

Yesterday, today, and tomorrow, I live and move in the one. Whatever I am feeling at any moment, I know that I am never alone. I know that the key thing is to live love, to work on this consciousness of living and projecting love in all my contacts with people. When I am, I will become loveable and loved. I will become attracted and socially acceptable. Opening the way for many friends and companions, until finally into this flow of relationships will ultimately come a special person with whom I can experience a memorable kind of mutual love.

I receive. I accept. I embrace.

Reflections:

Yesterday, today, and tomorrow, I live and move in the one. Whatever I am feeling at any moment, I know that I am never alone. I may not be able to help what I like, but I can help what I love because liking is a feeling. I know that love is the willingness to let love flow through me in the direction of my involvement.

I receive. I accept. I embrace.

Reflections:

January 30 **GOOD ORDERLY DIRECTION**

Yesterday, today, and tomorrow, I live and move in the one. Whatever I am feeling at any moment, I know that I am never alone. I know that I have dislikes for certain foods and have distastes for certain colors. I know that likes may be on many levels and may come and go, but love is my nature. When I am fulfilling the potential of my being, I express love to all persons. But if I say yes to love in the direction of some person I do not like, things will begin to happen; that person may ultimately become a friend.

I receive. I accept. I embrace.

Reflections: _____
_____
_____
_____
_____
_____

Yesterday, today, and tomorrow, I live and move in the one. Whatever I am feeling at any moment, I know that I am never alone. Many beautiful relationships never happen, simply because many do not exercise the freedom to love, thus releasing the possibility of a transcendent communion.

I receive. I accept. I embrace.

Reflections:

GOOD ORDERLY DIRECTION

FEBRUARY

Yellow Primroses

SELF APPRECIATION

Yesterday, today, and tomorrow, I live and move in the one. Whatever I am feeling at any moment, I know that I am never alone. I often ask myself, how do I see myself? I know that I do not see myself as a self-image that anyone else could give me, but the image in which I am created. Right now in this moment, I allow every cell and organ and function of my body to respond to it. I know that my physical heartbeat is probably different from anyone else. I know that my spiritual frequency, individually, is expressing as me, right in this moment, I appreciate myself.

I receive. I accept. I embrace.

Reflections: _____
_____
_____
_____
_____
_____

February 2 — **GOOD ORDERLY DIRECTION**

Yesterday, today, and tomorrow, I live and move in the one. Whatever I am feeling at any moment, I know that I am never alone. I appreciate myself. This is my uniqueness, and I know that there is one heartbeat in the universe. I know that each one of us expresses it uniquely. I know that this body, this temple in which I live, move and have my being is the first to feel it, right now in this moment. I give way to this spiritual frequency.

I receive. I accept. I embrace.

Reflections: _____
_____
_____
_____
_____
_____

Ayin M. Adams, Ph.D. February 3

Yesterday, today, and tomorrow, I live and move in the one. Whatever I am feeling at any moment, I know that I am never alone. Today, I resolve to walk in new ways. I know that as I put my hand in the hands of Spirit, my consciousness will be synchronized with the mind of the One Principle, the Almighty, instead of with the ways of the world. I walk by faith and not by sight, and my way will be paved with unbelievable good. I will walk with a spring in my step, which means I will walk in the paths of eternal springtime. I know that this will certainly be a wonderful year. Let's get still for just a moment.

I receive. I accept. I embrace.

Reflections: _____
_____
_____
_____
_____
_____

February 4 — **GOOD ORDERLY DIRECTION**

SPIRITUAL FREEDOM

Yesterday, today, and tomorrow, I live and move in the one. Whatever I am feeling at any moment, I know that I am never alone. I appreciate myself. I appreciate my uniqueness. I know that it is not an ego trip, it is responsibility, spiritual responsibility, and it also has spiritual freedom, to be me.

I receive. I accept. I embrace.

Reflections:

Yesterday, today, and tomorrow, I live and move in the one. Whatever I am feeling at any moment, I know that I am never alone. I know that this spiritual freedom to be me, calls me to look out into the world that is my environment, whether I call it Divine Order, it doesn't matter, but I know that that same rhythm of love and creativity is Presence, and I know that the Presence is present, meaning here and now.

I receive. I accept. I embrace.

Reflections:

February 6 — **GOOD ORDERLY DIRECTION**

Yesterday, today, and tomorrow, I live and move in the one. Whatever I am feeling at any moment, I know that I am never alone. If there is someone that I am praying for today, I know that I must go beyond the personal, I must go beyond the body, I must go beyond the outer appearances and know… the heartbeat of the universe is right here and I free you and everything that concerns you. I know that there is harmony everywhere, and I know it is now.

I receive. I accept. I embrace.

Reflections:

Yesterday, today, and tomorrow, I live and move in the one. Whatever I am feeling at any moment, I know that I am never alone. I know that when I get synchronized with the frequency of the universe, I know that there is abundance everywhere, and I live, move, and have my being in this frequency of universal love.

I receive. I accept. I embrace.

Reflections:

February 8 — **GOOD ORDERLY DIRECTION**

EMBRACING GOOD

Yesterday, today, and tomorrow, I live and move in the one. Whatever I am feeling at any moment, I know that I am never alone. I embrace my new awareness. I embrace my consciousness. I embrace the shift in my evolution. I embrace Goodness. I embrace the Source.

I receive. I accept. I embrace.

Reflections:

Yesterday, today, and tomorrow, I live and move in the one. Whatever I am feeling at any moment, I know that I am never alone. No longer am I content with setting things right. I embrace clarity. I know that the gift of clear seeing is the ability to see rightly. I see with eyes of love.

I receive. I accept. I embrace.

Reflections:

February 10 — **GOOD ORDERLY DIRECTION**

UNIVERSAL ENERGY

Yesterday, today, and tomorrow, I live and move in the one. Whatever I am feeling at any moment, I know that I am never alone. When I am out of focus, I know that the creative energy of love is the precise heart of the universe, beating individually as each one. I know the peace of being aligned with this spiritual frequency and resonating with it so thoroughly. This is a part of my own being-ness.

I receive. I accept. I embrace.

Reflections: _____
_____
_____
_____
_____

Ayin M. Adams, Ph.D. February 11

Yesterday, today, and tomorrow, I live and move in the one. Whatever I am feeling at any moment, I know that I am never alone. There is no separation. I am connected to one everywhere present heart. Each one of us is an individual heartbeat. I also know that peace of being is synchronized, of coming together. It is so much to listen too, to feel, to expand with. I know that it is right where I am, not some day, but right now, in the present moment.

I receive. I accept. I embrace.

Reflections:

February 12 — **GOOD ORDERLY DIRECTION**

PRAYER

Yesterday, today, and tomorrow, I live and move in the one. Whatever I am feeling at any moment, I know that I am never alone. I meditate and lift up my eyes and become one with all. I know that this is silent prayer. I know that by lifting up my eyes, I lift up my awareness. I lift up my consciousness and when I lift up my awareness and consciousness, I become synchronize. I now feel the frequency of the universe and I resonate with it, and this is my Oneness. This is my prayer.

I receive. I accept. I embrace.

Reflections:

Yesterday, today, and tomorrow, I live and move in the one. Whatever I am feeling at any moment, I know that I am never alone. How do I describe prayer? In human words, I know that to describe prayer, I would call it, the highest frequency of energy. I know that the truth of the matter is that, it doesn't matter what I call it, or how I describe it, they are just words. I know that it is the experience. It is not something I force, It already is me, and I do not ask for It, It is my spiritual nature.

I receive. I accept. I embrace.

Reflections:

February 14   **GOOD ORDERLY DIRECTION**

Yesterday, today, and tomorrow, I live and move in the one. Whatever I am feeling at any moment, I know that I am never alone. I know that prayer is quite simple. Prayer is one word, one word only. YES. And my prayer is done.

I receive. I accept. I embrace.

Reflections: _____
_____
_____
_____
_____
_____

BLESSINGS

Yesterday, today, and tomorrow, I live and move in the one. Whatever I am feeling at any moment, I know that I am never alone. I bless others, so that I may be a blessing upon myself. I teach so that I may lead. I dedicate this day to goodness. I bless my business and know the sacredness of all life is humility, community, and grace.

I receive. I accept. I embrace.

Reflections:

ENTERING THE STILLNESS

Yesterday, today, and tomorrow, I live and move in the one. Whatever I am feeling at any moment, I know that I am never alone. I get still and come to that center of my own being, coming to that place in consciousness where only I can go, that secret place, that sacred place. I know that as I close the door on everything in the outer, this time is for knowing me.

I receive. I accept. I embrace.

Reflections:

Yesterday, today, and tomorrow, I live and move in the one. Whatever I am feeling at any moment, I know that I am never alone. As I prepare to enter into the stillness, I know that this will be a period of deep listening. I know that my work is closing the door on everything in the outer and quieting my thoughts. I know that this stillness allow space for the deeper wisdom as my heart gives rise.

I receive. I accept. I embrace.

Reflections:

February 18 — **GOOD ORDERLY DIRECTION**

Yesterday, today, and tomorrow, I live and move in the one. Whatever I am feeling at any moment, I know that I am never alone. As I enter into the space of stillness, I humbly ask you to please join me in bringing to life the intention of moving towards Unity. I know that as we quiet our thoughts, integrate the changes, we are continually opening our hearts to love.

I receive. I accept. I embrace.

Reflections:

Yesterday, today, and tomorrow, I live and move in the one. Whatever I am feeling at any moment, I know that I am never alone. In the stillness, I feel the changes that are happening internally within my being, at a rapid frequency. I know that I must honor these changes and honor myself as I am gentle with myself. I know that I am in the stillness of expansion.

I receive. I accept. I embrace.

Reflections:

FEAR TO FAITH

Yesterday, today, and tomorrow, I live and move in the one. Whatever I am feeling at any moment, I know that I am never alone. I know that fear is the absence of faith.

> **F**orget
> **E**verything
> **A**nd
> **R**un

I know that I must:

> **F**ace
> **E**verything
> **A**nd
> **R**ecover

Uncover, recover, and discover the faith in me.

I receive. I accept. I embrace.

Reflections: _____
_____
_____
_____
_____
_____

Ayin M. Adams, Ph.D. February 21

Yesterday, today, and tomorrow, I live and move in the one. Whatever I am feeling at any moment, I know that I am never alone. I let go of doubt, distrust, worry and fear. I change the direction of my life by changing my thinking. I now move from fear to faith.

I receive. I accept. I embrace.

Reflections: _____
_____
_____
_____
_____
_____

MAKING LOVE

Yesterday, today, and tomorrow, I live and move in the one. Whatever I am feeling at any moment, I know that I am never alone. I ask that when I come together with my Divine partner in love, I know that our physical vessels are channels for the highest expression of love. I know that in this sacred activity of joy and bliss, we are coming together on all levels of our being: body, mind, spirit, and emotions. I know that our making love brings a continuation of love and light and a high frequency and vibration to the planet. And now, we move into the orgasmic flow of Oneness and sparkles and bright lights shine and beam throughout the world.

I receive. I accept. I embrace.

Reflections:

Yesterday, today, and tomorrow, I live and move in the one. Whatever I am feeling at any moment, I know that I am never alone. My closer connection to the One is at hand. I know that it is time to network with Heaven. I know that it is time to step up to the God realm. I know that in this realm, there is love, peace, and protection there.

I receive. I accept. I embrace.

Reflections:

February 24 — **GOOD ORDERLY DIRECTION**

SPIRITUAL ARMOR PRAYER

Yesterday, today, and tomorrow, I live and move in the one. Whatever I am feeling at any moment, I know that I am never alone. This is my prayer. This is my spiritual armor prayer that I must put on at this time on the earth plane. I pray my prayer over and over and over again until I feel the peace running through me. I make a conscious decision to forgive whoever, or whatever has done me wrong in my life. Whoever has ever let me down, I forgive and release the past. I forgive myself for any wrong choices that I have made.

I receive. I accept. I embrace.

Reflections: _____
_____
_____
_____
_____
_____

Ayin M. Adams, Ph.D.　　　　　　February 25

Yesterday, today, and tomorrow, I live and move in the one. Whatever I am feeling at any moment, I know that I am never alone. I speak my spiritual armor prayer until peace moves through my entire being. I ask the sacred precious spirit to come live inside me. And as I do, I receive restoration and feel that the power from Heaven is released into me. With this great power within me, all demonic spirits and thoughts that bother me are removed. They must go now. They must leave forever and immediately, for the river of healing is now. I know that sickness can no longer raise its ugly head, nor does fear raise its head. I know that God speaks peace into my spirit because my spiritual armor is on now. I know that I have been anointed, and I know that depending upon my faith it can and will move my mountains. I know that this truth has been given to me, and I now give it freely to others also in need. I will pray my prayer until I feel the peace running through me.

I receive. I accept. I embrace.

Reflections: _____
_____
_____
_____
_____
_____

February 26 — **GOOD ORDERLY DIRECTION**

Yesterday, today, and tomorrow, I live and move in the one. Whatever I am feeling at any moment, I know that I am never alone. During sleepless nights when I am awake, I bring my concerns to God. I speak to God about this. During the day, I check on myself at least twice and restore the calm by going to God and the tranquility that I am overlooking will come. And in all things, I give thanks.

I receive. I accept. I embrace.

Reflections:

Yesterday, today, and tomorrow, I live and move in the one. Whatever I am feeling at any moment, I know that I am never alone. As I undergo this change, a challenge of limitation, in the moment of greatest darkness, right now, I am aware of the light and I recognize the true creative powers that have been given to me. I recognize them at the moment of darkness. I know that I am being cautioned to restrain from any impulses linked with anger, and the impulse to do something that is linked with anger. I know that there is a beginning, middle, and an end that is always followed by another new beginning.

I receive. I accept. I embrace.

Reflections:

February 28 **GOOD ORDERLY DIRECTION**

Yesterday, today, and tomorrow, I live and move in the one. Whatever I am feeling at any moment, I know that I am never alone. Whatever disappointments I have experienced in my recent past, I must not allow myself to suffer over those recent sufferings. I also know that my experiences of the recent past have been a quickening of development for me and it has not gone unnoticed. My mind is stayed on good, God, the omnipotent.

I receive. I accept. I embrace.

Reflections: _____
_____
_____
_____
_____
_____

Yesterday, today, and tomorrow, I live and move in the one. Whatever I am feeling at any moment, I know that I am never alone. I become still. I wait to hear from God. I know that my prayers will be answered. I learn to wait upon God with patience. I pray and listen. I know that I will receive a word or I will be shown a vision. I wait with patience upon the will of Heaven.

I receive. I accept. I embrace.

Reflections:

GOOD ORDERLY DIRECTION

MARCH

Daffodil

CHOICES

Yesterday, today, and tomorrow, I live and move in the one. Whatever I am feeling at any moment, I know that I am never alone. Every moment, I am making a choice between love and fear, over and over and over again. I know that each choice that I make can connect me to unresolved fears or separation. I know that each choice I make can connect me to love and the harmony of oneness and togetherness. Today I know that the most powerful choice that I can ever make is my attitude.

I receive. I accept. I embrace.

Reflections:

March 2 — **GOOD ORDERLY DIRECTION**

Yesterday, today, and tomorrow, I live and move in the one. Whatever I am feeling at any moment, I know that I am never alone. I know that I am connected to everyone and we are connected to Oneness. When I feel overwhelmed by situations and challenges in my life, I know that I must look at the choices I have made. I know that when I make choices that empower me, I am making choices from a place of love, trust, and joy. I know that I am deliberately choosing to grow and unfold.

I receive. I accept. I embrace.

Reflections: _____
_____
_____
_____
_____
_____

Yesterday, today, and tomorrow, I live and move in the one. Whatever I am feeling at any moment, I know that I am never alone. When I claim that I have no choice, or I was given no choice, I know that this is a lie. The Truth is that I make choices in every present moment. I know that healthy choices support my evolution as I continue to grow and expand.

I receive. I accept. I embrace.

Reflections: _____
_____
_____
_____
_____
_____

March 4 — **GOOD ORDERLY DIRECTION**

Yesterday, today, and tomorrow, I live and move in the one. Whatever I am feeling at any moment, I know that I am never alone. I may not feel like I have a choice when I am caught up in the dramas of others' realities. I know that I always have a choice. I choose my attitude and I choose my thoughts. I choose to take responsibility for how I live my life. I know that I always have a choice, even when I may not believe it.

I receive. I accept. I embrace.

Reflections:

Ayin M. Adams, Ph.D. March 5

Yesterday, today, and tomorrow, I live and move in the one. Whatever I am feeling at any moment, I know that I am never alone. I choose to take responsibility by waking up! I know that when I choose to take responsibility, I am making a choice. I am now choosing to release others to take responsibility for themselves. I have a choice.

I receive. I accept. I embrace.

Reflections: _____
_____
_____
_____
_____
_____

March 6 — GOOD ORDERLY DIRECTION

Yesterday, today, and tomorrow, I live and move in the one. Whatever I am feeling at any moment, I know that I am never alone. I know that I have a choice. I choose me this day. I choose to serve my higher self. I now choose to expand my consciousness and lift my awareness to the level of the Divine without dragging the Divine down to human levels.

I receive. I accept. I embrace.

Reflections:

Yesterday, today, and tomorrow, I live and move in the one. Whatever I am feeling at any moment, I know that I am never alone. I choose to take responsibility for my little ones, thus showing them love by the power of example and in the demonstration of my actions. I love my children. I love myself.

I receive. I accept. I embrace.

Reflections:

March 8 — GOOD ORDERLY DIRECTION

Yesterday, today, and tomorrow, I live and move in the one. Whatever I am feeling at any moment, I know that I am never alone. If I believe that things will never change, it is a choice. I know that I am being called to listen more intently. I am being called to go within. I know that when I do listen, I am able to create changes within by my choices. The universe is demanding that I make choices based on my experiences.

I receive. I accept. I embrace.

Reflections: _____
_____
_____
_____
_____

March 9

Yesterday, today, and tomorrow, I live and move in the one. Whatever I am feeling at any moment, I know that I am never alone. I know that I am not a victim. I make healthy choices daily. I choose my path with every choice I make. I know that the best choices are made from my heart and what comes from the heart reaches the heart. I choose to live in this awareness.

I receive. I accept. I embrace.

Reflections:

March 10 — **GOOD ORDERLY DIRECTION**

Yesterday, today, and tomorrow, I live and move in the one. Whatever I am feeling at any moment, I know that I am never alone. I know that what is happening within me, I am ready to experience now. I know that I am willing to experience It now. I know that if It is there and It is moving through me, it is because I am ready and willing to know It, and to experience It, and to give It flow, which means: let It come forth. I know that It is a seed that is destined to bring forth flowers. And at this moment, right where I am, I am ready!

I receive. I accept. I embrace.

Reflections:

Yesterday, today, and tomorrow, I live and move in the one. Whatever I am feeling at any moment, I know that I am never alone. I know that I am important to the universe. I know that the universe chooses me this day to express as me and through me.

I receive. I accept. I embrace.

Reflections: _____
_____
_____
_____
_____
_____

March 12 — **GOOD ORDERLY DIRECTION**

CONTROLLING EMOTIONS

Yesterday, today, and tomorrow, I live and move in the one. Whatever I am feeling at any moment, I know that I am never alone. No longer do I allow emotions to control me. I have emotions, but I am not my emotions. I can control my emotions and rise above them to do tremendous good things in the world.

I receive. I accept. I embrace.

Reflections:

Yesterday, today, and tomorrow, I live and move in the one. Whatever I am feeling at any moment, I know that I am never alone. I know that in order to control my emotions I must first admit that I am experiencing emotional drives. I know that I must acknowledge the emotion and see where it leads me. I then surrender, stop defending, avoiding, blaming, and reacting to others' emotions. Finally, I remember that everything is in Divine Order, and when I can remember that, I am growing and evolving.

I receive. I accept. I embrace.

Reflections:

March 14 — **GOOD ORDERLY DIRECTION**

TRANSPARENCY

Yesterday, today, and tomorrow, I live and move in the one. Whatever I am feeling at any moment, I know that I am never alone. No longer do I just sit and wait to be caught in lies and to be uncovered through my selfish thoughtless actions. I know that I am being given a greater view of transparency in order to understand how my thoughts and actions affect others. We are all connected. The clarity of transparency will reveal all in one way or another. It is time to expose the truth. No longer am I content with hiding. I know that it is infinitely less painful to open myself to that transparency by being honest.

I receive. I accept. I embrace.

Reflections:

Ayin M. Adams, Ph.D. March 15

Yesterday, today, and tomorrow, I live and move in the one. Whatever I am feeling at any moment, I know that I am never alone. The veil is extremely thin. I know that I am living between two worlds; a world of reality and a world of non-reality. I know and fulfill my Divine purpose.

I receive. I accept. I embrace.

Reflections:

March 16   **GOOD ORDERLY DIRECTION**

CALL OF THE SOUL

Yesterday, today, and tomorrow, I live and move in the one. Whatever I am feeling at any moment, I know that I am never alone. When my soul calls, I answer. I know that this season brings a time to seek those who are in my spiritual soul energies. I know that this season I seek out my personal sanctuary and go deeper into my spirit.

I receive. I accept. I embrace.

Reflections:

Yesterday, today, and tomorrow, I live and move in the one. Whatever I am feeling at any moment, I know that I am never alone. When my soul calls, I answer. I know that it is time to form my own spiritual group and my special place in sacred Iao Valley. I connect to those souls and partners with whom I feel great to be around. I extend myself to the vibrational places in which to do my spiritual work.

I receive. I accept. I embrace.

Reflections:

March 18 — **GOOD ORDERLY DIRECTION**

Yesterday, today, and tomorrow, I live and move in the one. Whatever I am feeling at any moment, I know that I am never alone. I know my purpose for being here on the earth. I am blessed to be alive at such an incredible time in this world which has change, challenge, and is filled with opportunities. I must remain diligent, focused, and centered in the Divine flow of love. I remain grounded at all times.

I receive. I accept. I embrace.

Reflections:

Yesterday, today, and tomorrow, I live and move in the one. Whatever I am feeling at any moment, I know that I am never alone. Although I may be at a standstill right now, I know that this halt is felt because of the growth I am experiencing along with my difficulties. I know that the steadfastness of my will is important. I meditate and pray throughout my awake time. I constantly have God on my lips and on my mind as I go about my day. Communing with God and constantly walking and talking with God lifts my consciousness and keeps me in alignment.

I receive. I accept. I embrace.

Reflections:

March 20 — GOOD ORDERLY DIRECTION

Yesterday, today, and tomorrow, I live and move in the one. Whatever I am feeling at any moment, I know that I am never alone. I can never be afraid of anything or anyone when I have an open doorway to Heaven. I have communication with the God-head. The door is open to me. I can go in and out of this door to communicate with God. I have fellowship with God. My fellowship is strong with God. I can ask for guidance. I can ask questions beforehand and get answers. This is all by total faith and communication. I am walking with the CEO. By my faith it is done. By my faith, it is accomplished. By my faith I receive. By my faith all is well. All comes forth by faith and faith alone.

I receive. I accept. I embrace.

Reflections:

Yesterday, today, and tomorrow, I live and move in the one. Whatever I am feeling at any moment, I know that I am never alone. My faith is being tested. I know that power is given from God to me, and the arm of God is extraordinarily long and reaches into every tiny crevice. My faith is being tested. True faith stands the testing and to such is given the key to Heaven. All is and will be given to those who stand the testing of true faith. I am such a one.

I receive. I accept. I embrace.

Reflections:

March 22 — GOOD ORDERLY DIRECTION

Yesterday, today, and tomorrow, I live and move in the one. Whatever I am feeling at any moment, I know that I am never alone. As I grow through emotional pain, I know that I must bring the pain into the light. Whether it is founded in a relationship, family, financial or loss of any kind, I know that I must keep my faith firm. I step back, breathe, and tune in with my higher self in all matters of the heart. I create harmony in my world.

I receive. I accept. I embrace.

Reflections: _____
_____
_____
_____
_____

Yesterday, today, and tomorrow, I live and move in the one. Whatever I am feeling at any moment, I know that I am never alone. I must not be anxious when plans are put on hold for a while. I move into the quietness of being still. Peace be still. During this time, I know that my renewal is at the core of my soul's deepest level. I open my eyes to watch for signs of spring when things become alive again.

I receive. I accept. I embrace.

Reflections:

March 24 — GOOD ORDERLY DIRECTION

Yesterday, today, and tomorrow, I live and move in the one. Whatever I am feeling at any moment, I know that I am never alone. No longer do I lie to myself. I get honest and ask myself the difficult questions: Is it wealth I desire or possession? Is it self-rule I seek? I know that I am my own boss. I need not answer to any human. I simply pray; Dear God, show me the correct way. Lord, I will walk in your footprints. I will walk behind you.

I receive. I accept. I embrace.

Reflections:

Yesterday, today, and tomorrow, I live and move in the one. Whatever I am feeling at any moment, I know that I am never alone. Even though the time looks like bad fortune I do not give in to it. I do not give in to the emotions; I control my emotions. I control the highs as well as the lows. I know that healthy behavior is needed. I know that there is Divine right action. I do not escape by denying right action. I do not feel dismay. When there is a dilemma of right action to take or which way to turn, left or right, I know that diligence is called forth. When I examine what has occurred and I examine my role, I can look at my needs and the needs of other people. I am strong and courageous. I meditate day and night.

I receive. I accept. I embrace.

Reflections: _____
_____
_____
_____
_____
_____

March 26 — **GOOD ORDERLY DIRECTION**

Yesterday, today, and tomorrow, I live and move in the one. Whatever I am feeling at any moment, I know that I am never alone. When I reflect back over the panorama of my life, accountability for harms cause, real or imagined, I make peace with my past. Rather than accounting for specific wrongs, I look at the sum total of my life and in its simplest form. I let go I let flow. I let go I let flow.

I receive. I accept. I embrace.

Reflections: _____
_____
_____
_____
_____

Yesterday, today, and tomorrow, I live and move in the one. Whatever I am feeling at any moment, I know that I am never alone. The easiest thing in the world for two people is to fall in love. It is easy for two lonely people who are hungering for a relationship to fall in love. I know that falling in love is a romantic fantasy. In most cases it is a falling from love into an unsettling, emotional frenzy. Two people tend to fall in love, but fall out of the Divine flow into an emotional, physical, even sexual feeling.

I receive. I accept. I embrace.

Reflections:

March 28   **GOOD ORDERLY DIRECTION**

Yesterday, today, and tomorrow, I live and move in the one. Whatever I am feeling at any moment, I know that I am never alone. I know that love is not two people looking goo-goo eyed at each other. Rather love is two people looking out the same window together seeing the same thing. I know that true love is two people who are first of all friends, who enjoy playing the game of life together and with one another, and celebrate their lives together. This is a beautiful true form of love.

I receive. I accept. I embrace.

Reflections: _____
_____
_____
_____
_____
_____

Yesterday, today, and tomorrow, I live and move in the one. Whatever I am feeling at any moment, I know that I am never alone. It is sad to see two people swept up into a relationship, married or unmarried, reaching a crisis in the post honeymoon stages where they awaken to the realization that they are not close friends. This is startling and surprising, yet this is the impermanent nature of human feelings.

I receive. I accept. I embrace.

Reflections:

March 30   **GOOD ORDERLY DIRECTION**

Yesterday, today and tomorrow, I live and move in the one, whatever I am feeling at any moment, I know that I am never alone. My life today is about the quality of my relationship to myself. With all my minor failures, setbacks, and disappointments, it is the quality of my relationship to self. I do not place value in what others are saying about me. I do not think this way.

I receive. I accept. I embrace.

Reflections: _____
_____
_____
_____
_____
_____

PROBLEMS

Yesterday, today, and tomorrow, I live and move in the one. Whatever I am feeling at any moment, I know that I am never alone. No longer do I try to fight my way through problems, to beg or cheat my way through. I know that it is only when I think my way through that I begin to find answers. Of course, I can pray my way through. I know that prayer is thought on a higher perspective, high level thinking, and transcendental thinking.

I receive. I accept. I embrace.

Reflections:

GOOD ORDERLY DIRECTION

APRIL

Yellow Daisies

SEEING BEYOND APPEARANCES

Yesterday, today, and tomorrow, I live and move in the one. Whatever I am feeling at any moment, I know that I am never alone. When I train my eyes to see beyond appearances, I see Spirit present. I see Good present. I see simplistic solutions to answers. I am calm and at peace with myself, the world, and everyone in it.

I receive. I accept. I embrace.

Reflections:

April 2 — GOOD ORDERLY DIRECTION

Yesterday, today, and tomorrow, I live and move in the one. Whatever I am feeling at any moment, I know that I am never alone. I know that I am a channel becoming the full expression of God.

I receive. I accept. I embrace.

Reflections: _____
_____
_____
_____
_____
_____

Yesterday, today, and tomorrow, I live and move in the one. Whatever I am feeling at any moment, I know that I am never alone. As I become still and come to that center of my own being, I am aware that during these few moments I have opened my consciousness to a new expansion; one that only I can experience, one that I can say yes to, one that I am ready for. I know that the universe always say yes to me. I know that I will forever let my life echo yes, yes, yes.

I receive. I accept. I embrace.

Reflections:

April 4 — **GOOD ORDERLY DIRECTION**

Yesterday, today, and tomorrow, I live and move in the one. Whatever I am feeling at any moment, I know that I am never alone. Whatever I need comes to me. Spirit never says no. I know that there is never an answer of no in infinite Mind, only eternal yes. I say yes to my good. I know that I am moving with the movement of creativity. I am so grateful.

I receive. I accept. I embrace.

Reflections:

CHANGE

Yesterday, today, and tomorrow, I live and move in the one. Whatever I am feeling at any moment, I know that I am never alone. Although the feelings of giving birth to a new awareness has been challenging, I know that I've completed a 180 degree breakthrough in the process of self- change. I went beyond the change. The change has been made. I know that trust has been involved, and it has been made. I know that the darkness is behind me. I am not finished with the work. I know that hard work is still ahead for me.

I receive. I accept. I embrace.

Reflections: _____
_____
_____
_____
_____
_____

April 6 — **GOOD ORDERLY DIRECTION**

LIVING IN THE NOW

Yesterday, today, and tomorrow, I live and move in the one. Whatever I am feeling at any moment, I know that I am never alone. No longer do I collapse myself into thoughts of the future. I live in the moment. No longer do I jump into the future. I live in the moment of now.

I receive. I accept. I embrace.

Reflections: _____
_____
_____
_____
_____
_____

April 7

Yesterday, today, and tomorrow, I live and move in the one. Whatever I am feeling at any moment, I know that I am never alone. As I live in the present moment I stand still. I know that this is my time for standing still. No longer do I feel a sense of powerlessness. I surrender to the now. I surrender to the moment of now. I stand still. I live in the now.

I receive. I accept. I embrace.

Reflections:

April 8 — GOOD ORDERLY DIRECTION

Yesterday, today, and tomorrow, I live and move in the one. Whatever I am feeling at any moment, I know that I am never alone. In this sacred moment of now, I am patient. I know that I must grow my seed to give birth. I am holding on. I am be… ing…still in the moment.

I receive. I accept. I embrace.

Reflections: _____
_____
_____
_____
_____
_____

Yesterday, today, and tomorrow, I live and move in the one. Whatever I am feeling at any moment, I know that I am never alone. If my good is stuck, or if there is a detour I know that I must stand still and hang on. I know that my good is coming as I sit in the moment of now and trust the process as it unfolds. I know that union and reunion will manifest. I trust the now.

I receive. I accept. I embrace.

Reflections:

April 10 — **GOOD ORDERLY DIRECTION**

MOVEMENT

Yesterday, today, and tomorrow, I live and move in the one. Whatever I am feeling at any moment, I know that I am never alone. If a desired outcome that I am waiting for eludes me if there is a blockage, I know that this is a re-routing opportunity. I see this as a sign of movement, forward movement.

I receive. I accept. I embrace.

Reflections:

Yesterday, today, and tomorrow, I live and move in the one. Whatever I am feeling at any moment, I know that I am never alone. If my good is stuck or detoured I know that it is coming, I watch for signs of spring to manifest. This too is forward movement. I know that opportunity comes effortlessly. These are signs that things are moving again, not standing still.

I receive. I accept. I embrace.

Reflections:

April 12 — **GOOD ORDERLY DIRECTION**

PATIENCE

Yesterday, today, and tomorrow, I live and move in the one. Whatever I am feeling at any moment, I know that I am never alone. No longer am I anxious about events. I know that events may interfere with growth, but I also know that in the end, the destination is what I desire. This is what I want. It will be good. I know that diligence is required at this time. I allow things to unfold in Spirit time not my time. Patience is required of me.

I receive. I accept. I embrace.

Reflections:

Yesterday, today, and tomorrow, I live and move in the one. Whatever I am feeling at any moment, I know that I am never alone. Patience is required of me. By letting things unfold I know that this is the desired outcome of what I came upon the earth to do. I am patient.

I receive. I accept. I embrace.

Reflections:

April 14 — **GOOD ORDERLY DIRECTION**

CLARITY

Yesterday, today, and tomorrow, I live and move in the one. Whatever I am feeling at any moment, I know that I am never alone. I know that my biggest challenge is clarity. If I am not clear I am ambiguous. The most important thing is having clarity and having a correct relationship with myself.

I receive. I accept. I embrace.

Reflections:

FOCUS

Yesterday, today, and tomorrow, I live and move in the one. Whatever I am feeling at any moment, I know that I am never alone. No longer am I letting worldly events be my main focus. No longer do I follow nonsense. I know that I must be in the world yet not of it. I see the world around me. I am not a part of that herd. I know that I must remain focused on a sense of my true direction, a sense to follow my blueprint.

I receive. I accept. I embrace.

Reflections:

April 16 — GOOD ORDERLY DIRECTION

Yesterday, today, and tomorrow, I live and move in the one. Whatever I am feeling at any moment, I know that I am never alone. I know that many are distracted at this present time, and many will continue to be distracted. Many are not doing their work. I must keep the focus on myself. I know that Spirit has given me vision so that I do not get off the path.

I receive. I accept. I embrace.

Reflections:

Yesterday, today, and tomorrow, I live and move in the one. Whatever I am feeling at any moment, I know that I am never alone. No longer do I lose focus. I am content to do my task, especially without always seeking credit. I know that I have a plan with God. I know that I have a list of things to accomplish. I know that I have a list of goals to get done before coming to earth. And I know that I still want to follow my blueprint.

I receive. I accept. I embrace.

Reflections:

April 18 — GOOD ORDERLY DIRECTION

Yesterday, today, and tomorrow, I live and move in the one. Whatever I am feeling at any moment, I know that I am never alone. As I continue to remain focused, I am also remaining faithful, quiet, and mindful. I am the perfect peace of tranquility. I continue with trust, and I continue with perseverance.

I receive. I accept. I embrace.

Reflections:

Yesterday, today, and tomorrow, I live and move in the one. Whatever I am feeling at any moment, I know that I am never alone. I know that extraordinary faith must have great trials. I know that strength will be born in the midst of the storm. I pray: "With God in my boat. I smile at the storm."

I receive. I accept. I embrace.

Reflections:

April 20   **GOOD ORDERLY DIRECTION**

INTIMACY

Yesterday, today, and tomorrow, I live and move in the one. Whatever I am feeling at any moment, I know that I am never alone. Intimacy is self-discovery and self-discovery is inner work to do. I discover the loving woman that I am today, yesterday, and who I will become tomorrow.

I receive. I accept. I embrace.

Reflections:
_____
_____
_____
_____
_____
_____

DISCOVERY

Yesterday, today, and tomorrow, I live and move in the one. Whatever I am feeling at any moment, I know that I am never alone. If I do not love and appreciate myself who will? I am worthy because I am and for no other reason. I know that discovery of joy, peace, love, laughter, and kindness is work to be done in me. It is my inner work. I discover about myself that I do not allow others to dictate my life or actions.

I receive. I accept. I embrace.

Reflections:

April 22 — **GOOD ORDERLY DIRECTION**

ACCEPTANCE

Yesterday, today, and tomorrow, I live and move in the one. Whatever I am feeling at any moment, I know that I am never alone. I _____ accept my Divine position in the universe and take sole responsibility as a Divine sacred _____.

I receive. I accept. I embrace.

Reflections: _____

Yesterday, today, and tomorrow, I live and move in the one. Whatever I am feeling at any moment, I know that I am never alone. I accept the fact that I may not be able to change what happens to me, but I can change what happens within me and I can change how I respond to things that happen in my world. I accept in order to heal.

I receive. I accept. I embrace.

Reflections:

April 24 — **GOOD ORDERLY DIRECTION**

Yesterday, today, and tomorrow, I live and move in the one. Whatever I am feeling at any moment, I know that I am never alone. I accept myself completely and wholly without blame, shame, guilt, or judgment. I know that when I empower myself, I honor myself. I express my brilliance. I practice my faith. I show my courage, and this makes me happy.

I receive. I accept. I embrace.

Reflections:

PAIN

Yesterday, today, and tomorrow, I live and move in the one. Whatever I am feeling at any moment, I know that I am never alone. Whether I experience family pain, relationship pain, job pain or other pains, I know that pain teaches me and brings me into the consciousness of now. Inside the now is my true longing for self. I know that it is not a suffering. It is an undergoing of change.

I receive. I accept. I embrace.

Reflections:

April 26 — **GOOD ORDERLY DIRECTION**

DEATH

Yesterday, today, and tomorrow, I live and move in the one. Whatever I am feeling at any moment, I know that I am never alone. Death shakes one up to one's very core. I am aware of how short life is. I know that I must examine myself and know where I am going in the spirit and where I will end up in the spirit. I am consciously waking up myself, family, and friends. I know that death is an on-going process. Wake up and ask the questions: Where am I going? What am I truly seeking?

I receive. I accept. I embrace.

Reflections:

LIGHT

Yesterday, today, and tomorrow, I live and move in the one. Whatever I am feeling at any moment, I know that I am never alone. I know that I've always had this special light. Humbly, I open myself more and more and allow the light that has been kept secret. My prayer is simply: Spirit, you who are the source of all power, whose ray of light illuminates the world. Illuminate also my heart, so that it too can do your work. As I offer my prayer, I feel the love coming in and out of me, permeating my being. I feel a warm feeling entering me, and this warm feeling saturates my spirit and absorbs like a sponge.

I receive. I accept. I embrace.

Reflections:

April 28   **GOOD ORDERLY DIRECTION**

Yesterday, today, and tomorrow, I live and move in the one. Whatever I am feeling at any moment, I know that I am never alone. As I continue to illuminate my heart with Spirit's help I pray, lifting up my consciousness to the Divine. I am soaking my spirit deeply and frequently. I know that my spirit and soul must be saturated and filled up. I know that my cup is full. I know that I have plenty to give to others. I now use it to heal others, anoint others, move mountains and teach others to move mountains. My spirit is now so full that it is illuminated and others see it.

I receive. I accept. I embrace.

Reflections:

Yesterday, today, and tomorrow, I live and move in the one. Whatever I am feeling at any moment, I know that I am never alone. I know that life can be surprising and challenging. I know that life is also to be looked at it in wonderment. My life goal is to remain stress free. I stop worrying about things which leads to non- belief in God. God is looking and saying, "Why? I have it covered for you." Today I wake up and say, "I am not worrying about this; it has already been taken care of."

I receive. I accept. I embrace.

Reflections:

HEALING

Yesterday, today, and tomorrow, I live and move in the one. Whatever I am feeling at any moment, I know that I am never alone. All powers have been given me. I speak with the authority of one who knows. I ask for forgiveness of any wrong doings. I welcome the powers that be to enter into my spirit, to stay, and to work with me. I place my hands over my eyes and speak the powerful words of healing out loud with deep feeling, meaning, and sincerity. I know that I can take on any ailment and release it. This is the healing power within me. I remember this always.

I receive. I accept. I embrace.

Reflections: _____
_____
_____
_____
_____
_____

Ayin M. Adams, Ph.D.

GOOD ORDERLY DIRECTION

MAY

Lily of the Valley

Yesterday, today, and tomorrow, I live and move in the one. Whatever I am feeling at any moment, I know that I am never alone. I know that nobody likes the one that knows the truth. It is either face the truth or go back into denial. I bless you on your way. Thank you for providing me with this opportunity to learn. I release you and let you go. I know that in the end, I will be okay.

I receive. I accept. I embrace.

Reflections: _____
_____
_____
_____
_____
_____

May 2 — **GOOD ORDERLY DIRECTION**

Yesterday, today, and tomorrow, I live and move in the one. Whatever I am feeling at any moment, I know that I am never alone. I know what these feelings are telling me. These feelings are expressing through me that the peace within me is ready to be brought up out of the darkness and into the light. I send love and healing to myself. I bless my path.

I receive. I accept. I embrace.

Reflections:

Yesterday, today, and tomorrow, I live and move in the one. Whatever I am feeling at any moment, I know that I am never alone. I know that I cared a little about you. I know that I got overly involved. I know that you have received enough from me for the moment. I know that you received wisdom from me, and it lies within you. I bless you, and I let you go.

I receive. I accept. I embrace.

Reflections:

May 4 — **GOOD ORDERLY DIRECTION**

Yesterday, today, and tomorrow, I live and move in the one. Whatever I am feeling at any moment, I know that I am never alone. I know that I've started the opening for you. This is done. It is finished. I'm moving on. I wish you well, and I bless you on your way. I know that by letting you go, I am honoring your process. I know that if I do not I am forcing you into making decisions about what is right or not. I honor you as you process and progress. I hold the space that is high and good for you. But I let you go now. I know that I gave you the capabilities. Spirit thank you for presenting me with people to help. I'll take a breather now.

I receive. I accept. I embrace.

Reflections:

Yesterday, today, and tomorrow, I live and move in the one. Whatever I am feeling at any moment, I know that I am never alone. I want you to know that what you have said or done to me was not intentional. I took it personally. I got synchronized with it. I now know that my energy is too important to become synchronized with energy that is not in harmony with mine. I have allowed you to stop my blessings. I forgive you. I now realize that by forgiving you, I am taking back my powers. Right here and right now, in this moment, I am free.

I receive. I accept. I embrace.

Reflections:

May 6 — GOOD ORDERLY DIRECTION

Yesterday, today, and tomorrow, I live and move in the one. Whatever I am feeling at any moment, I know that I am never alone. I know that I must heal myself and others through forgiveness, when I find myself over-reacting to situations, especially in relationships. I know that when I am experiencing difficulty receiving or giving love, that it is time to go within, to find the answers.

I receive. I accept. I embrace.

Reflections:
___
___
___
___
___

Yesterday, today, and tomorrow, I live and move in the one. Whatever I am feeling at any moment, I know that I am never alone. I know that when I learn to love myself I will attract healthier relationships, healing, and blessings from the universe. I know that not only does self-love heals, but so does love received from others. I practice loving myself.

I receive. I accept. I embrace.

Reflections:

May 8   **GOOD ORDERLY DIRECTION**

Yesterday, today, and tomorrow, I live and move in the one. Whatever I am feeling at any moment, I know that I am never alone. When I experience love I know that I am resonating with the essence of the universe and who I am. I know that loving self involves accepting love and care from others as well as loving myself.

I receive. I accept. I embrace.

Reflections:

Yesterday, today, and tomorrow, I live and move in the one. Whatever I am feeling at any moment, I know that I am never alone. The truth is that I can only give what I have. If I do not love and accept myself unconditionally, I cannot truly love and accept you either.

I receive. I accept. I embrace.

Reflections:

May 10   **GOOD ORDERLY DIRECTION**

Yesterday, today, and tomorrow, I live and move in the one. Whatever I am feeling at any moment, I know that I am never alone. I am not speaking from ego. I know that ego means **E**asing **G**od **O**ut. I know that I am talking about valuing myself and full acceptance of myself. I know this because I exist, I am worthy, and I am a part of the Divine Rivers of flowing life.

I receive. I accept. I embrace.

Reflections:

Yesterday, today, and tomorrow, I live and move in the one. Whatever I am feeling at any moment, I know that I am never alone. I know that learning to love myself is one of the greatest gifts that I can give myself and others. I know that love heals the physical, the mental, and the spiritual. Love is a three-fold balm. I know that love is my nature and that we are all one.

I receive. I accept. I embrace.

Reflections:
_____
_____
_____
_____
_____
_____

May 12 **GOOD ORDERLY DIRECTION**

Yesterday, today, and tomorrow, I live and move in the one. Whatever I am feeling at any moment, I know that I am never alone. One of the greatest gifts that I can give myself is self-acceptance. Accepting myself means that I know how to love myself in spite of my character defects and shortcomings. I know that I am okay with myself and my body no matter what. Say this truth with me: "I love myself no matter what. I love myself no matter what."

I receive. I accept. I embrace.

Reflections:

Yesterday, today, and tomorrow, I live and move in the one. Whatever I am feeling at any moment, I know that I am never alone. I know that I need to stay with these feelings and to feel what I am feeling. I know that feelings are not facts, but it is a fact that I feel. When I am awake, aware, and alert, I know that these levels transform and shift my energy.

I receive. I accept. I embrace.

Reflections:

May 14   **GOOD ORDERLY DIRECTION**

TRUST

Yesterday, today, and tomorrow, I live and move in the one. Whatever I am feeling at any moment, I know that I am never alone. As I continue to rely on trust, I gain in prosperity. I know that achievement and success come along with this trust. This is my call to a new life and it is unfolding. I expect the unexpected. I gain a new sense of solidarity with the Divine.

I receive. I accept. I embrace.

Reflections: _____
_____
_____
_____
_____
_____

PRIDE AND PRESUMPTION

Yesterday, today, and tomorrow, I live and move in the one. Whatever I am feeling at any moment, I know that I am never alone. No longer do I resist God. I know that pride and presumption is what can keep me from hearing God. I know that Spirit resists the proud and gives to the humble. Today, I keep my pride and presumption in check.

I receive. I accept. I embrace.

Reflections:

LOVE

Yesterday, today, and tomorrow, I live and move in the one. Whatever I am feeling at any moment, I know that I am never alone. I know that I am part of this love light. No longer do I single myself out. I am content to feel the entire flow of love. I am going places and doing things. I am a part of this big family of love.

I receive. I accept. I embrace.

Reflections:

Yesterday, today, and tomorrow, I live and move in the one. Whatever I am feeling at any moment, I know that I am never alone. No longer do I waste energy foolishly and lust after a desired outcome. I know that patience is needed. I know that perseverance is needed.

I receive. I accept. I embrace.

Reflections:

May 18 — GOOD ORDERLY DIRECTION

Yesterday, today, and tomorrow, I live and move in the one. Whatever I am feeling at any moment, I know that I am never alone. No longer am I eager to press forward. I know that this is not a time to press forward. This is not a time to push my influence. I know that patience is needed. I embrace and exhibit patience.

I receive. I accept. I embrace.

Reflections:
_____
_____
_____
_____
_____

Yesterday, today, and tomorrow, I live and move in the one. Whatever I am feeling at any moment, I know that I am never alone. No longer am I seduced by my old ways. I know that difficulties can and will arise at the beginning of my new life. I know that this time is for my fruit to ripen on the branch. I am patient. I observe and take the high road. I set my house in order. I give up my old ways, while waiting for the new to begin.

I receive. I accept. I embrace.

Reflections:

May 20   **GOOD ORDERLY DIRECTION**

Yesterday, today, and tomorrow, I live and move in the one. Whatever I am feeling at any moment, I know that I am never alone. No longer do I welcome trouble. I set my house in order by not borrowing trouble. No longer do I have strife. No longer do I worry. I know that worry means I have no faith whatsoever. Today, I change the channel of my thoughts.

I receive. I accept. I embrace.

Reflections:

CREATIVE WAITING

Yesterday, today, and tomorrow, I live and move in the one. Whatever I am feeling at any moment, I know that I am never alone. Sometimes I want what I want when I want it, and usually I want it right now. I know that the ability to wait a while and to accept immediate frustrations in order to achieve a future gain is one of the marks of a mature mentality and emotions.

I receive. I accept. I embrace.

Reflections:

GOOD ORDERLY DIRECTION

Yesterday, today, and tomorrow, I live and move in the one. Whatever I am feeling at any moment, I know that I am never alone. I know that it is an indication of insecurity or immaturity to have to have what you want or else to refuse to play the game. What is true in the realm of the mental is certainly true in the realm of the spirit. Waiting is an important part of communion that I call prayer. Faith presupposes an interval of patiently waiting. I wait with intelligence, with love, with imagination, and with joy. This is what it means to wait creatively.

I receive. I accept. I embrace.

Reflections:

Yesterday, today, and tomorrow, I live and move in the one. Whatever I am feeling at any moment, I know that I am never alone. I know that to wait with all the right attributes of right thinking is to wait creatively. Creative waiting is one of the secrets to answered prayer.

I receive. I accept. I embrace.

Reflections: _____
_____
_____
_____
_____
_____

May 24 — GOOD ORDERLY DIRECTION

Yesterday, today, and tomorrow, I live and move in the one. Whatever I am feeling at any moment, I know that I am never alone. I've been guilty at one time thinking of waiting as a period of inactivity. I know now that waiting is not a dull sterile period of inactivity. Waiting is not passive at all. Waiting is defined as a "state of being," that which occupies my time and attention. Waiting can be a Divine occupation.

I receive. I accept. I embrace.

Reflections: _____
_____
_____
_____
_____
_____

Yesterday, today, and tomorrow, I live and move in the one. Whatever I am feeling at any moment, I know that I am never alone. I turn to the Bible for further revelation on the subject of creative waiting. I find that waiting is not only an occupation, but a very worthwhile occupation. In Isaiah, I read, "Jehovah is a God of justice; blessed are they that wait for him." It is in Romans that I get a deeper insight into the heart of the matter: "For in hope we were saved, but hope that is seen is not hope, for who hoped for that which he see, but if we hope for that which we see not, then we with patience wait for it."

I receive. I accept. I embrace.

Reflections:

May 26 — GOOD ORDERLY DIRECTION

Yesterday, today, and tomorrow, I live and move in the one. Whatever I am feeling at any moment, I know that I am never alone. I know that waiting is the child of hope and the very Mother of faith. I no longer need authentic proof. I know that waiting is a desirable state of being occupied. It is a God-given respite during which the hidden things of life are nurtured, before they are brought into outer manifestation.

I receive. I accept. I embrace.

Reflections:

Yesterday, today, and tomorrow, I live and move in the one. Whatever I am feeling at any moment, I know that I am never alone. No longer do I rush into relationships. It is okay to be with myself and wait in this fertile period. I experience a new growth and flowering of my inner self. I know that by taking time for myself, I will be ready to awaken to the growth of a beautiful, gentle, and loving relationship.

I receive. I accept. I embrace.

Reflections:

GOOD ORDERLY DIRECTION

Yesterday, today, and tomorrow, I live and move in the one. Whatever I am feeling at any moment, I know that I am never alone. Once my seeds have been planted, they must not be uprooted and replanted again and again by dubious repetition. I know that I must learn to wait upon Spirit or wait upon the will of Heaven.

I receive. I accept. I embrace.

Reflections:

Yesterday, today, and tomorrow, I live and move in the one. Whatever I am feeling at any moment, I know that I am never alone. I know that many a love has been ruined by poking around at its roots. The same may happen in my spiritual garden as in my earthly experiences. Today, I learn not to poke around at its roots, lest the development of my seed and love be stunted by impatience, forgetfulness of the Divine resource, the meaning, and the Divine plan of unfoldment.

I receive. I accept. I embrace.

Reflections:

May 30 — GOOD ORDERLY DIRECTION

Yesterday, today, and tomorrow, I live and move in the one. Whatever I am feeling at any moment, I know that I am never alone. I am told that, "except a grain of wheat fall into the earth and die, it abides by itself alone, but if it dies, it bears much fruit." This is a wonderful, hidden truth of dying in order to live, of giving to receive, of letting go in order to hold on, of hiding in order to manifest. I know that this is how I am to give my desires and my manifestations over to the Divine flow. I must hide them in Spirit. Next I let them die in Spirit's will and purpose, so that they will live again in a Divine and planned manifestation!

I receive. I accept. I embrace.

Reflections:

Yesterday, today, and tomorrow, I live and move in the one. Whatever I am feeling at any moment, I know that I am never alone. I know that it is not always about me. I know that my relationship with another must be based on a spiritual union when I can truly let go of myself, truly let go of my personal wants, and selfish urges.

I receive. I accept. I embrace.

Reflections:

GOOD ORDERLY DIRECTION

JUNE

White Roses

Yesterday, today, and tomorrow, I live and move in the one. Whatever I am feeling at any moment, I know that I am never alone. I know that I am the Kingdom. I know that I am in tune with that Kingdom that longs to express through me, through my hands, through my thoughts, through my work, into my family, and out into my world.

I receive. I accept. I embrace.

Reflections:

June 2 — **GOOD ORDERLY DIRECTION**

Yesterday, today, and tomorrow, I live and move in the one. Whatever I am feeling at any moment, I know that I am never alone. I know that I am part of a Divine plan. Within me is the seed that longs to bear its perfect fruit as me, abundantly and joyously.

I receive. I accept. I embrace.

Reflections:

Yesterday, today, and tomorrow, I live and move in the one. Whatever I am feeling at any moment, I know that I am never alone. That which is me cannot be taken away by anyone. It can never be severed. It can never be lost. It can never grow old. I know that It is always the eternal me and It is always complete in Spirit.

I receive. I accept. I embrace.

Reflections:

June 4 — **GOOD ORDERLY DIRECTION**

Yesterday, today, and tomorrow, I live and move in the one. Whatever I am feeling at any moment, I know that I am never alone. When good things happen to me, it does not mean that I now feel good because something good has happened to me. Something good has happened to me because I have already found the good within myself.

I receive. I accept. I embrace.

Reflections: _____
_____
_____
_____
_____

Yesterday, today, and tomorrow, I live and move in the one. Whatever I am feeling at any moment, I know that I am never alone. This is my life to live. This is my unfoldment to allow. There is a flow that longs to unfold through me and flow through me. There is a world out there waiting to be created through me.

I receive. I accept. I embrace.

Reflections:

June 6 — GOOD ORDERLY DIRECTION

Yesterday, today, and tomorrow, I live and move in the one. Whatever I am feeling at any moment, I know that I am never alone. This world that is waiting to be created through me, I do not see as something separate from me. I know that the world calls it commercial, the world calls it a job, you can call it what you will. I see it as an unfoldment of that Divine source, of that Divine idea, of that abundance, of that joy. I know that it is the creative word coming forth, creating, creating, and creating through me.

I receive. I accept. I embrace.

Reflections:
_____
_____
_____
_____
_____
_____

Yesterday, today, and tomorrow, I live and move in the one. Whatever I am feeling at any moment, I know that I am never alone. I know that with each word that I speak, with each idea that I give birth to, with each unfoldment that I am part of, I grow. And I begin to know more deeply and more profoundly than ever, my true identity, my oneness, and my wholeness.

I receive. I accept. I embrace.

Reflections:

June 8   **GOOD ORDERLY DIRECTION**

Yesterday, today, and tomorrow, I live and move in the one. Whatever I am feeling at any moment, I know that I am never alone. I know my true name today. It is a name that is a seed that is destined to bring forth flowers. And at this moment right where I am…I am ready.

I receive. I accept. I embrace.

Reflections: _____
_____
_____
_____
_____
_____

Yesterday, today, and tomorrow, I live and move in the one. Whatever I am feeling at any moment, I know that I am never alone. I know myself. I respect my divinity. I accept my inheritance. I make my commitment, and I am joyous of the responsibility that comes with spiritual fulfillment.

I receive. I accept. I embrace.

Reflections:

June 10 — GOOD ORDERLY DIRECTION

Yesterday, today, and tomorrow, I live and move in the one. Whatever I am feeling at any moment, I know that I am never alone. I have come for a time such as this. I know the fullness of time is right now. With a new energy and a new freedom to go forth and be, I say yes. I listen quietly to the inner celebration of joy. And it is done. So be it.

I receive. I accept. I embrace.

Reflections: _____
_____
_____
_____
_____

SADNESS

Yesterday, today, and tomorrow, I live and move in the one. Whatever I am feeling at any moment, I know that I am never alone. No longer do I hold on to sadness. I know that Spirit desires me to be rid of it. I know that I no longer need sadness. Spirit teaches me how to hold on to these gifts and keep what is given to me, especially wonderful things.

I receive. I accept. I embrace.

Reflections:

June 12 — GOOD ORDERLY DIRECTION

Yesterday, today, and tomorrow, I live and move in the one. Whatever I am feeling at any moment, I know that I am never alone. No longer do I need sadness. I know that my old ways have been in my own way, and I lost many gifts that have been given to me. I know that I don't always hold on to them and this causes sadness. I now hold the blessings that have been given to me and will continue to be given to me.

I receive. I accept. I embrace.

Reflections:

CLARITY

Yesterday, today, and tomorrow, I live and move in the one. Whatever I am feeling at any moment, I know that I am never alone. No longer are my thoughts cluttered. I am clear on my intent. I know that if it doesn't feel right I just wait. I know that I must have clear thoughts first. I must wait on the will of Heaven. I know that powerful forces of change are at work. I know and feel that gains and rewards that I did not anticipate are in the Divine plan. I am of clear thoughts and make my decisions.

I receive. I accept. I embrace.

Reflections: _____
_____
_____
_____
_____
_____

June 14 — **GOOD ORDERLY DIRECTION**

Yesterday, today, and tomorrow, I live and move in the one. Whatever I am feeling at any moment, I know that I am never alone. When I face challenges, tests, frustrations, or when I am helping other people, I dip into my pool to divert defeat. I pull deeply into my reservoir of inner strength. I know that I have a deep pool from which to draw from. I dip into the pool of reserve.

I receive. I accept. I embrace.

Reflections: _____
_____
_____
_____
_____
_____

PRAYER

Yesterday, today, and tomorrow, I live and move in the one. Whatever I am feeling at any moment, I know that I am never alone. All illness, physical, emotional, mental, must leave me now forever. For the rivers of healing is now. I speak peace into my Spirit. I know that sickness can no longer raise its ugly head. My armor is now on. I have been anointed. Faith is needed to know this. Truth is given to me.

I receive. I accept. I embrace.

Reflections:

June 16 — GOOD ORDERLY DIRECTION

Yesterday, today, and tomorrow, I live and move in the one. Whatever I am feeling at any moment, I know that I am never alone. No longer do I pray to God. I now pray with God. I pray from God. I know that this is a very important significant spiritual insight, because my prayer is simply letting God be God in me. I know that God's word takes the form of inspiration and aspiration. I pray from my consciousness of God.

I receive. I accept. I embrace.

Reflections: _____
_____
_____
_____
_____
_____

Yesterday, today, and tomorrow, I live and move in the one. Whatever I am feeling at any moment, I know that I am never alone. I know that the very act of prayer is an activity of God. Listen, pray, and move your feet. I know that the moving of my feet becomes a vital part of the prayer process. It is the action step. I also know that I have free will. I become so still that the activity of goodness can move me and set me on the path to success which is the perfect path for me.

I receive. I accept. I embrace.

Reflections:

June 18 — GOOD ORDERLY DIRECTION

Yesterday, today, and tomorrow, I live and move in the one. Whatever I am feeling at any moment, I know that I am never alone. No longer am I trying to fix things. I do not need to solve problems and seek things to be right. I do not need to change my partner, change the children, or even myself. To try and fix things usually means that I am looking for the quick fix. When I see something that I do not like it means that I am trying to fix it, I am trying to change it. I know that it is much important to me today to try and understand it.

I receive. I accept. I embrace.

Reflections: _____
_____
_____
_____
_____
_____

Yesterday, today, and tomorrow, I live and move in the one. Whatever I am feeling at any moment, I know that I am never alone. I know that I am spiritual in nature and human in experience. It is good to know this about myself. I also know that I have a built in yearning to fulfill my potential as a Divine soul of love.

I receive. I accept. I embrace.

Reflections:

SEX WITHOUT LOVE

Yesterday, today, and tomorrow, I live and move in the one. Whatever I am feeling at any moment, I know that I am never alone. I know that to engage in sex without love, without a love commitment is to function on almost an animal level of being. Sex without love can lead only to emptiness and loneliness. One may cover up his/her emptiness by boasting of his/her love life and love conquests, but in reality one can meaninglessly go from one experience to another seeking in sex that which can only be found in love.

I receive. I accept. I embrace.

Reflections:

Yesterday, today, and tomorrow, I live and move in the one. Whatever I am feeling at any moment, I know that I am never alone. I know that I am much more than just a sexual animal. I am potentially a Divine creature. Through universal love, I am raised from a biological organism to the level of my divinity. And I know that it is only through love that I can become creative, self-disciplined, and realize my true human potential.

I receive. I accept. I embrace.

Reflections:

GOOD ORDERLY DIRECTION
June 22

Yesterday, today, and tomorrow, I live and move in the one. Whatever I am feeling at any moment, I know that I am never alone. A true relationship, whether married or unmarried, must be a union of peers, in which there is no need for dominance, subjection, submission or downright stifling possessiveness. I know that a relationship must be based on mutual caring and trust, so that each partner has the freedom to be an individual.

I receive. I accept. I embrace.

Reflections:

Yesterday, today, and tomorrow, I live and move in the one. Whatever I am feeling at any moment, I know that I am never alone. In a healthy mutually loving relationship, each person is free to develop at his/her own pace. Though he/she grows as a separate person, through supportive love for one another, the union will grow stronger and richer.

I receive. I accept. I embrace.

Reflections: _____
_____
_____
_____
_____
_____

June 24 — GOOD ORDERLY DIRECTION

Yesterday, today, and tomorrow, I live and move in the one. Whatever I am feeling at any moment, I know that I am never alone. I know that the most humble act is being mindful and thoughtful of myself. When I look carefully at associations that I have formed it is important to remain conscious of those who are using me. Today I take responsibility and realize that I knew they were taking advantage of me. My objective is to take heart and learn from what has been taking place.

I receive. I accept. I embrace.

Reflections:

REGENERATION

Yesterday, today, and tomorrow, I live and move in the one. Whatever I am feeling at any moment, I know that I am never alone. I am cautious not to retreat into a repressed situation, especially if I am being pressed. I know that my regeneration goes down to my cellular level. I allow the light to balance and center me.

I receive. I accept. I embrace.

Reflections:

June 26   **GOOD ORDERLY DIRECTION**

ENERGY

Yesterday, today, and tomorrow, I live and move in the one. Whatever I am feeling at any moment, I know that I am never alone. I need not allow others to impose their negativity into my energy field. I know that I must remain in alignment with my energy. I welcome it. I greet it. I own it. I cultivate oneness. I dissolve any negativity that is going on in my own energy field.

I receive. I accept. I embrace.

Reflections:

Yesterday, today, and tomorrow, I live and move in the one. Whatever I am feeling at any moment, I know that I am never alone. I have taken you to my large bed and laid you in my warm embrace. I have drunk the sweet nectar from your river. Why do you question my love so?

I receive. I accept. I embrace.

Reflections:

June 28 — GOOD ORDERLY DIRECTION

Yesterday, today, and tomorrow, I live and move in the one. Whatever I am feeling at any moment, I know that I am never alone. To be honest with myself it is good to police myself and give myself a test that may prove to be somewhat shocking. I have to ask myself truthfully if I enjoy the other person or if I enjoy myself by using the other person. By truthfully being authentic, I know that the first is the enjoyment of love, and the second is the enjoyment of lust. When I am honest with myself I gain a better understanding of myself.

I receive. I accept. I embrace.

Reflections: _____
_____
_____
_____
_____
_____

Yesterday, today, and tomorrow, I live and move in the one. Whatever I am feeling at any moment, I know that I am never alone. When I enjoy myself with and through my partner, I know that we do not meet as persons, we meet as spirits of ourselves. So our pleasure is a spiritual pleasure that begins to satisfy the Divine soul.

I receive. I accept. I embrace.

Reflections:

June 30 — GOOD ORDERLY DIRECTION

Yesterday, today, and tomorrow, I live and move in the one. Whatever I am feeling at any moment, I know that I am never alone. I know that relationships that are not based on a lasting deep commitment to one another usually ends in misery. I know that in most cases, there is no real coming together, other than a sexual union. If I enjoy myself through the use of the other person, then there is a lot of subtle selfishness going on. This means that we relate on a lower level and I am unwilling to give of myself completely.

I receive. I accept. I embrace.

Reflections: _____
_____
_____
_____
_____
_____

Ayin M. Adams, Ph.D.

GOOD ORDERLY DIRECTION

JULY

Waterlily

Yesterday, today, and tomorrow, I live and move in the one. Whatever I am feeling at any moment, I know that I am never alone. I do not allow people to think for me. If someone presents me with an idea in which I totally disagree I think to myself, "Alright, that's what you think, but I choose to think differently. I am poised and centered in the mind of Infinite within me and none of these things move me. I am in tune with the Divine flow, and I think what I want to think. I think creatively. I think from within."

I receive. I accept. I embrace.

Reflections:

July 2 — **GOOD ORDERLY DIRECTION**

Yesterday, today, and tomorrow, I live and move in the one. Whatever I am feeling at any moment, I know that I am never alone. I know that my thoughts are not produced by conditions. My thoughts are shaped by the way I choose to deal with conditions, whether it is from a high or low perspective.

I receive. I accept. I embrace.

Reflections:

Yesterday, today, and tomorrow, I live and move in the one. Whatever I am feeling at any moment, I know that I am never alone. I know that I am wise only if I can correlate knowledge into consciousness where it improves the true level of my life. I know that this is the difference between the wise and the learned. One may have many facts but the other one knows the truth with which the facts deal only superficially. Emmanuel Kemp once said, "Science is organized knowledge, wisdom is organized life."

I receive. I accept. I embrace.

Reflections:

July 4 — GOOD ORDERLY DIRECTION

Yesterday, today, and tomorrow, I live and move in the one. Whatever I am feeling at any moment, I know that I am never alone. I know that I do not have to always try to reason things out. Instead, I am willing to let go, to listen, and to let the Infinite mind flow forth. I allow Spirit Mind to think through me. I am an intuitive person. I let this inner guidance lead me into ways of richness, fineness, and fullness. I know that this is willingness instead of will, mind attunement instead of mind control.

I receive. I accept. I embrace.

Reflections: _____
_____
_____
_____
_____
_____

Yesterday, today, and tomorrow, I live and move in the one. Whatever I am feeling at any moment, I know that I am never alone. I know that the spirit in me is me. I am spirit. I do not have to become spiritual, I am spiritual. I know that any attempt to become spiritual may lead to pasting on a lot of religious axioms and bottling up of basic emotions and intellectual perceptions.

I receive. I accept. I embrace.

Reflections:

July 6 **GOOD ORDERLY DIRECTION**

Yesterday, today, and tomorrow, I live and move in the one. Whatever I am feeling at any moment, I know that I am never alone. Today I am freely me. I stand in my own power. I no longer give my power away to people, places or things in exchange for scraps of approval, love, or security. I know that this is my moment of truth.

I receive. I accept. I embrace.

Reflections:

ACCEPTING SELF

Yesterday, today, and tomorrow, I live and move in the one. Whatever I am feeling at any moment, I know that I am never alone. I no longer have to constantly find out what others are doing or where others are hanging out. I no longer try to get something for nothing or avoid someone or something. I know that when I accept myself, I am okay, and it is okay to be me.

I receive. I accept. I embrace.

Reflections: _____
_____
_____
_____
_____
_____

July 8 — GOOD ORDERLY DIRECTION

Yesterday, today, and tomorrow, I live and move in the one. Whatever I am feeling at any moment, I know that I am never alone. I know that struggling to be me will not work. The world will never change to meet my ideas and conditions. Therefore, I need to change my mind to meet conditions in the world, whatever they may be. I know that the choice is mine. I accept myself for who I am. I live my life from within-out, not from without- in.

I receive. I accept. I embrace.

Reflections:

WITNESS

Yesterday, today, and tomorrow, I live and move in the one. Whatever I am feeling at any moment, I know that I am never alone. I am no longer easily agitated with disturbing feelings. I know that when I sit as witness, I am comfortable with myself. I simply sit and observe what is happening within my being. I release, and I let go. I relax as witness and all disturbances flee. I know that as I give rise to Spirit energies flowing in, these energies lift me up and bring me joy, love, and peaceful feelings.

I receive. I accept. I embrace.

Reflections:

July 10   **GOOD ORDERLY DIRECTION**

Yesterday, today, and tomorrow, I live and move in the one. Whatever I am feeling at any moment, I know that I am never alone. I know that by practicing being a witness, I allow Spirit energy to permeate my being. The more Spirit energy I have at my disposal the more Spirit I feel. The more I want to control things my way, the less I feel Spirit. I know that when I accept myself, I come to love myself, and I know that this is what I desire all along. This makes it easier to navigate this world.

I receive. I accept. I embrace.

Reflections:

SPIRITUAL BLUE PRINT

Yesterday, today, and tomorrow, I live and move in the one. Whatever I am feeling at any moment, I know that I am never alone. I know that if I had chosen to bare children, I would never accomplish what I want to do this lifetime. I would have stayed home and taken care of my children. I am with myself to accomplish what is in my blue print. I know that my blue print will not deter me or take away from what I need to get done. I have raised countless children and helped thousands of souls through my contacts with them. I have connected hundreds of thousands of people together, and that work has been a part of my blue print. I am happy and content with performing my spiritual life work.

I receive. I accept. I embrace.

Reflections: _____
_____
_____
_____
_____
_____

July 12   **GOOD ORDERLY DIRECTION**

RELATIONSHIPS

Yesterday, today, and tomorrow, I live and move in the one. Whatever I am feeling at any moment, I know that I am never alone. I know that if I list all the relationships I have had, all the people I have touched and gotten to know and grow with, it is more than those individuals with 30 years of marriage. I know that I have not been neglected in this sense. I must remember this truth.

I receive. I accept. I embrace.

Reflections:

Yesterday, today, and tomorrow, I live and move in the one. Whatever I am feeling at any moment, I know that I am never alone. I know that it is not about finding the right person but being the right person. When I am being the right person, I naturally attract the right people into my life.

I receive. I accept. I embrace.

Reflections:

July 14   **GOOD ORDERLY DIRECTION**

INVITING SPIRIT

Yesterday, today, and tomorrow, I live and move in the one. Whatever I am feeling at any moment, I know that I am never alone. I pray, "God, please forgive any wrong doings I have done, real or imagined. Please come into my Spirit to stay and work with me."

I receive. I accept. I embrace.

Reflections:

LET GO/LET FLOW

Yesterday, today, and tomorrow, I live and move in the one. Whatever I am feeling at any moment, I know that I am never alone. No longer do I mourn for losing that which is not for my highest good. Today I know that everything is transient and passes away. The only constant is God's love. I let go, I let flow.

I receive. I accept. I embrace.

Reflections: _____
_____
_____
_____
_____
_____

July 16 — GOOD ORDERLY DIRECTION

Yesterday, today, and tomorrow, I live and move in the one. Whatever I am feeling at any moment, I know that I am never alone. There is no need to hold on. I let go, I let flow. I send love, light, and healing to those who are in pain and conflict. I know that they are not angry with me but upset with letting go and allowing the changes of life to take place.

I receive. I accept. I embrace.

Reflections:

GREATER FREEDOM

Yesterday, today, and tomorrow, I live and move in the one. Whatever I am feeling at any moment, I know that I am never alone. I stand at the door of greater freedom and I knock, knowing that all that I seek opens to me and calls me to life's fullness. My decision to accept my greater freedom is a greater power within me. I can call it God, Buddha, Allah, Creator, Intelligence, or Source. Whatever I may call it, I know that It is greater than myself and leads me to greater freedom.

I receive. I accept. I embrace.

Reflections:

July 18 — GOOD ORDERLY DIRECTION

Yesterday, today, and tomorrow, I live and move in the one. Whatever I am feeling at any moment, I know that I am never alone. I stand at the door of greater freedom and I knock, knowing that this greater freedom leads me, directs me and guides me. I am undaunted by challenges that I face. I have courage. I know that my Divine self will never fail me, because I know that I am in tune with Spirit and out of step with the world. I know that when I leap the net will always appear.

I receive. I accept. I embrace.

Reflections: _____
_____
_____
_____
_____
_____

Yesterday, today, and tomorrow, I live and move in the one. Whatever I am feeling at any moment, I know that I am never alone. New beginnings are before me. I am reminded to continue to discipline myself. I know that I must carve out sacred time and devote myself to my spiritual practices.

I receive. I accept. I embrace.

Reflections:

July 20 — GOOD ORDERLY DIRECTION

Yesterday, today, and tomorrow, I live and move in the one. Whatever I am feeling at any moment, I know that I am never alone. There is a great shift deep within my being. I am remaining in love. Without trust, I know that trust will not resonate.

I receive. I accept. I embrace.

Reflections:

FORWARD MOVEMENT

Yesterday, today, and tomorrow, I live and move in the one. Whatever I am feeling at any moment, I know that I am never alone. No longer do I unconsciously avoid things or situations that rise up in my consciousness. I know that there is that within me which is bigger than the challenge, bigger than the crisis or situation. I possess the tools in which to meet life and life's pressing concerns. I move forward.

I receive. I accept. I embrace.

Reflections:

GOOD ORDERLY DIRECTION

Yesterday, today, and tomorrow, I live and move in the one. Whatever I am feeling at any moment, I know that I am never alone. No longer do I unconsciously avoid things that enter my consciousness. I know that when I address what annoys me. I will heal my life. I know that I am not always right, but neither am I always wrong. This is my time for being humble. This time calls me to breathe. As I breathe I can see where my breath is leading me. I follow the flow of my heart.

I receive. I accept. I embrace.

Reflections:

BLOCKAGES

Yesterday, today, and tomorrow, I live and move in the one. Whatever I am feeling at any moment, I know that I am never alone. Whenever I am experiencing physical blockages in the body whether the pain is in the back, neck, arm, eyes, or anywhere else, I know that I am undergoing a passage. I know that whatever the blockage is, it will not last long. This experience is a deep passage down to my cellular level. It is a rite of passage. I restrain myself from running to clinics.

I receive. I accept. I embrace.

Reflections:

July 24   GOOD ORDERLY DIRECTION

Yesterday, today, and tomorrow, I live and move in the one. Whatever I am feeling at any moment, I know that I am never alone. Whenever my movement appears blocked I know that movement is blocked for a reason. Through an inner awareness I know that not all possibilities are open to me, because all opportunities are not appropriate for me.

I receive. I accept. I embrace.

Reflections: _____
_____
_____
_____
_____
_____

WHOLENESS

Yesterday, today, and tomorrow, I live and move in the one. Whatever I am feeling at any moment, I know that I am never alone. I know that I am already whole. I seek after that which I am: wholeness. I bring my essence down into the cellular level of my being. I know that it is love that lives through me.

I receive. I accept. I embrace.

Reflections:

BELOVED

Yesterday, today, and tomorrow, I live and move in the one. Whatever I am feeling at any moment, I know that I am never alone. Past lives like we have overtaken us. It is so powerful. There is memory. There is an unusual meeting between us from past lives. Let us play it out. Spirit is offering us an opportunity. There is the memory of us. Deep inside you there is the memory of me. It is a pull I feel for you and a pull you feel for me. There is the memory of us. The memory of we. The memory of the beloved. Let us pursue us.

I receive. I accept. I embrace.

Reflections:

WISDOM

Yesterday, today, and tomorrow, I live and move in the one. Whatever I am feeling at any moment, I know that I am never alone. I don't always trust my own wisdom, but I know that I got it. I got wisdom. No longer do I need to ask others, "What do you think," when I know it all along. I regain my strength. Today I draw upon my own wisdom. Spirit says I have wisdom and instinct. I got it! I got wisdom!

I receive. I accept. I embrace.

Reflections:

July 28 — GOOD ORDERLY DIRECTION

Yesterday, today, and tomorrow, I live and move in the one. Whatever I am feeling at any moment, I know that I am never alone. The basis of any relationship between people is the willingness to share or the willingness to give. I must be authentic and ask myself, "What am I willing to give or give up?

I receive. I accept. I embrace.

Reflections:

Yesterday, today, and tomorrow, I live and move in the one. Whatever I am feeling at any moment, I know that I am never alone. No matter how much it may hurt I know that if I'm realistic I'll realize that there are some gifts that I cannot afford to give. It is very important that I see this. I may come to realize that my partner's well-being may necessitate things in which I do not want to spend time, money, or energy. In order words, I must know my limits. And it is okay to have limits. I cannot hide them under the banner of romantic love if that is the case.

I receive. I accept. I embrace.

Reflections:

July 30 — GOOD ORDERLY DIRECTION

Yesterday, today, and tomorrow, I live and move in the one. Whatever I am feeling at any moment, I know that I am never alone. The reason why many unmarried relationships do not fulfill or survive is that the partner does not make a commitment to the other's person's well-being, only to his/her own. Consequently, the you and me and the yours and mine never quite become the us and ours.

I receive. I accept. I embrace.

Reflections: _____
_____
_____
_____
_____
_____

Yesterday, today, and tomorrow, I live and move in the one. Whatever I am feeling at any moment, I know that I am never alone. This is for the person who is yearning to find his/her true partner, or for the one who is already married and involved in a satisfying relationship. I know that a true partner is not a new person to be met, but a new depth to be discovered in one's self.

I receive. I accept. I embrace.

Reflections:

GOOD ORDERLY DIRECTION

AUGUST

Orange Gladiolas

A NEW DAY

Yesterday, today, and tomorrow, I live and move in the one. Whatever I am feeling at any moment, I know that I am never alone. When I listen to that inner voice stirring within me that only I can hear, I will know that a new day has begun. I can see and hear how beautifully nature echoes truth.

I receive. I accept. I embrace.

Reflections:

| August 2 | **GOOD ORDERLY DIRECTION** |

Yesterday, today, and tomorrow, I live and move in the one. Whatever I am feeling at any moment, I know that I am never alone. When I think of the sunrise (the new day, the light of a new day, awakening me), I realize my inner light that has always been shining brightly. And every time I take a moment to be aware of it, to acknowledge it, and to experience it, it is as if I am moving into a new day of understanding. It is an expanding awareness resonating with my own self, my uniqueness, and my divinity.

I receive. I accept. I embrace.

Reflections: _____
_____
_____
_____
_____
_____

Yesterday, today, and tomorrow, I live and move in the one. Whatever I am feeling at any moment, I know that I am never alone. I know that this new dawn is my radiant light. It is my consciousness awakening in me at this very moment and it is very good.

I receive. I accept. I embrace.

Reflections:

August 4 — GOOD ORDERLY DIRECTION

Yesterday, today, and tomorrow, I live and move in the one. Whatever I am feeling at any moment, I know that I am never alone. I know that as I think about my physical mother, the best gift that I can give her is to free her to her own experience at the dawning of a new day, her own inner experience, her own inner freedom accepting in her that which is always nurturing her.

I receive. I accept. I embrace.

Reflections:

Yesterday, today, and tomorrow, I live and move in the one. Whatever I am feeling at any moment, I know that I am never alone. I know that I have had many people in my life who have mothered me and nurtured me. Wherever they are in Spirit I can say thank you. I recognize more than I ever did who and what they are. I am grateful. Thank you!

I receive. I accept. I embrace.

Reflections:

August 6 — **GOOD ORDERLY DIRECTION**

IN THE SILENCE

Yesterday, today, and tomorrow, I live and move in the one. Whatever I am feeling at any moment, I know that I am never alone. Without the distractions of so many things vying for my attention, especially my thoughts, as I move into the silence I listen and read only what is written in my heart. I know that it is the distraction of speech whether I write it, hear it, or speak it. That sacred silent space is so precious to me just as I am. I am extremely precious and beautifully vulnerable. I move into the silence.

I receive. I accept. I embrace.

Reflections:

Yesterday, today, and tomorrow, I live and move in the one. Whatever I am feeling at any moment, I know that I am never alone. In this sacred silent space it calls me to a slow conscious response to life, rather than a hurried anxious flow that I am accustomed to. I live, move, and have my being in the One. Join me as I allow myself the gift of silence in my heart space. I am always in the present where time does not exist. I am only aware of the here and now.

I receive. I accept. I embrace.

Reflections:

August 8 — **GOOD ORDERLY DIRECTION**

Yesterday, today, and tomorrow, I live and move in the one. Whatever I am feeling at any moment, I know that I am never alone. I suit up in the right attire. I show up at the designated place, and I follow through regardless of what's happening within me. I suit up, I show up, I follow through.

I receive. I accept. I embrace.

Reflections:

Yesterday, today, and tomorrow, I live and move in the one. Whatever I am feeling at any moment, I know that I am never alone.

Meditation Song: In the Silence

In the silence there is a sacred place,
a secret meeting place, Love is there.
In the silence, where every color blends,
and every rainbow ends, God is there.

In the silence there is a golden light,
it is peaceful and it is bright, Love is there.
In the silence, I'm drawn into the light,
I see a better life, no more doubt and fear.

In the silence there is a still small voice,
it is giving me a choice between love and fear.
In the silence the streets are paved with gold,
and no one's growing old, and God is there.

In the silence you live in light of Gold,
and all your dreams unfold, love is there.
In the silence where every color blends,
and every rainbow ends, God is there.

I receive. I accept. I embrace.

August 10 — **GOOD ORDERLY DIRECTION**

PRAYERS

Yesterday, today, and tomorrow, I live and move in the one. Whatever I am feeling at any moment, I know that I am never alone. "God, I am open now to receiving thy wisdom, to receiving thy will. I am open also for that portion of the self in which I am in complete unison with you. And so it is. Amen!"

I receive. I accept. I embrace.

Reflections:

Yesterday, today, and tomorrow, I live and move in the one. Whatever I am feeling at any moment, I know that I am never alone. "God, I am grateful. I am grateful for knowing. I am grateful for the Oneness that I have complete and total trust in you on the earth plane. And so it is then! Amen."

I receive. I accept. I embrace.

Reflections:

August 12 — **GOOD ORDERLY DIRECTION**

Yesterday, today, and tomorrow, I live and move in the one. Whatever I am feeling at any moment, I know that I am never alone. "God, I am open now to thy Divine and Infinite wisdom. I am also open to the fullness of my own spirit. I ask that I be used in ways for the greatest good of all upon the earth plane. I ask that I would receive and also to give forth. I ask that there would be blessings bestowed upon those with whom I interact and that they grow in acknowledgement of thy Divine light. And so it is, Amen."

I receive. I accept. I embrace.

Reflections:

Yesterday, today and tomorrow, I live and move in the one, whatever I am feeling at any moment I know that I am never alone. I ask myself, "How do I feel about myself, my character? This experience is a test of character. How do I feel? I know that I must stay centered as the answer rises up within my being, "I did my best. I did well."

I receive. I accept. I embrace.

Reflections:

August 14 — GOOD ORDERLY DIRECTION

Yesterday, today, and tomorrow, I live and move in the one. Whatever I am feeling at any moment, I know that I am never alone. I know that when I look at my thoughts and feelings, I know that there is no separation, there is still one energy, one heartbeat, one Divine Intelligence, expressing uniquely as me. I know that everything truly is in Divine order.

I receive. I accept. I embrace.

Reflections:

PRESSURE

Yesterday, today, and tomorrow, I live and move in the one. Whatever I am feeling at any moment, I know that I am never alone. Remember the old adage, "When things get tight, something's got to give." This statement means that the chain is no stronger than the weakest link. For example, in the midst of conflict, I could experience a nervous breakdown, hit the ceiling, lose my job, or experience some kind of tragic loss. I know that the pressure I have experienced is an inner build up resulting from how I deal with things. Today, I change my attitudes and become non-resistant by releasing the pressure and growing stronger.

I receive. I accept. I embrace.

Reflections:

August 16 — GOOD ORDERLY DIRECTION

Yesterday, today, and tomorrow, I live and move in the one. Whatever I am feeling at any moment, I know that I am never alone. As far as pressure is concerned I realize that one's enemies (negative thoughts) are in his/her own household. No longer am I content to allow these enemies to take up space rent free in my head. I know that no matter what happens out there in the world, or even what sits at my doorstep, all that ever really counts is what happens within my own mind. As I turn my thoughts to positive and my mind to peace, I know that nothing can or will disturb me.

I receive. I accept. I embrace.

Reflections:

Yesterday, today, and tomorrow, I live and move in the one. Whatever I am feeling at any moment, I know that I am never alone. No longer do I allow pressure to build up. When I am centered within myself, when I am centered in the Divine flow, life becomes an easier walk through experiences in the outer world with less conflict or pressure. But if I lose this inner center I become immersed with things at the circumference of life out there; I will be pushed and pulled and I will feel lost because I have no roots.

I receive. I accept. I embrace.

Reflections:

August 18   **GOOD ORDERLY DIRECTION**

REALIZATION

Yesterday, today, and tomorrow, I live and move in the one. Whatever I am feeling at any moment, I know that I am never alone. A most powerful realization is knowing that when I am centered within myself I know that I'm in charge. Neither the clock, the calendar, worldly priorities, the urge to conform, the fear of the future or the worry over the implication of the past, the cost of living, or the threat of recession are in charge. I am centered within myself and I am in charge. And the world may have its' pressures, but I can cope.

I receive. I accept. I embrace.

Reflections:

Yesterday, today, and tomorrow, I live and move in the one. Whatever I am feeling at any moment, I know that I am never alone. When the experience comes up in my heart, I must let it pass right through. I do not need to hold onto it whether it is good or incomplete. This is what human experience is all about. As I give way to the experience and let go of the anxiety about time, effort, how much, and when, I experience an easy and effortless unfoldment of all that is needed to be done. I can do the task one step at a time.

I receive. I accept. I embrace.

Reflections:

August 20 — GOOD ORDERLY DIRECTION

Yesterday, today, and tomorrow, I live and move in the one. Whatever I am feeling at any moment, I know that I am never alone. I love this realization: I work without strain and walk without hurrying, for I am in tune with the rhythm of the universe. That which needs to be done will be accomplished at the right and perfect time, in a right and perfect way and I will know. I believe that I am plugged into a Divine rhythm, and I can complete the tasks at hand without pressure.

I receive. I accept. I embrace.

Reflections:

Yesterday, today, and tomorrow, I live and move in the one. Whatever I am feeling at any moment, I know that I am never alone. When I am resisting change and fighting time, I may be dealing with people who are under a different set of priorities. When I become too involved in things that I am doing and goals that I am working for, I can act as if life begins and ends with getting a job, or getting a promotion, or meeting a deadline which keeps me under constant pressure. I let go. I no longer get caught up, I simply let go.

I receive. I accept. I embrace.

Reflections:

August 22 — GOOD ORDERLY DIRECTION

Yesterday, today, and tomorrow, I live and move in the one. Whatever I am feeling at any moment, I know that I am never alone. No longer am I out of step. I now know and believe that I am plugged into a Divine rhythm. I know that I can perform my tasks at hand without any pressure. I know that it is okay to have a plan and to keep it in the back of my mind. No longer do I worry about it or allow it to become an obsession. I know that this moment is all I have to work with. The past is behind me, and the future is yet to come.

I receive. I accept. I embrace.

Reflections: _____
_____
_____
_____
_____
_____

Ayin M. Adams, Ph.D. August 23

Yesterday, today, and tomorrow, I live and move in the one. Whatever I am feeling at any moment, I know that I am never alone. No longer am I preoccupied with foolishness. I know that my goal is not a preoccupation with tomorrow but a direction for the day. I know that in order to protect myself from the sense of pressure that comes from anxiety or the fear of failure I must be sure to keep myself now-minded. I must stay in the now and keep my magnifying mind off the future or the past.

I receive. I accept. I embrace.

Reflections:

August 24 **GOOD ORDERLY DIRECTION**

Yesterday, today, and tomorrow, I live and move in the one. Whatever I am feeling at any moment, I know that I am never alone. No longer am I impatient with myself and others. I have learned to be patient with myself and to give myself a loving pat on the back. I know that I have all eternity to achieve the goal. I know that part of spiritual growth is the experience of joy which I certainly sacrifice, if I sadly press on under the pressures to be perfect. I must do my best and leave the rest. And the latter is the important key, leave the rest, let it go. Do what I can, let it go, and relax. I free myself from all kinds of pressures which build up.

I receive. I accept. I embrace.

Reflections: _____
_____
_____
_____
_____
_____

Yesterday, today, and tomorrow, I live and move in the one. Whatever I am feeling at any moment, I know that I am never alone. In finding new depth to be discovered in myself, I need to make a new commitment to finding the Divine level within myself. And to the degree that I do this, I will draw to me a supportive relationship or draw the supportive love from a present relationship.

I receive. I accept. I embrace.

Reflections:

August 26 — GOOD ORDERLY DIRECTION

Yesterday, today, and tomorrow, I live and move in the one. Whatever I am feeling at any moment, I know that I am never alone. When two people really love each other they can deal with difficulties and even be blessed by them. Because in resolving their difficulties they become more aware of their likenesses. When two people are committed to the great expression of love and working together, then their desire to grow will help them grow together.

I receive. I accept. I embrace.

Reflections: _____
_____
_____
_____
_____
_____

Yesterday, today, and tomorrow, I live and move in the one. Whatever I am feeling at any moment, I know that I am never alone. Two people who grow together will become more involved in likeness than difference. I know that there will always be differences because people must be individuals. I also know that where there are no differences, there must be some indifference and that's dangerous.

I receive. I accept. I embrace.

Reflections:

August 28 — **GOOD ORDERLY DIRECTION**

FAITH

Yesterday, today, and tomorrow, I live and move in the one. Whatever I am feeling at any moment, I know that I am never alone. I take a moment for clarity and realize that whatever I am experiencing at any moment, "this too shall pass." When it does pass I will emerge from the darkened tunnel into the light and my life will never be experienced in the same way again. I know that I am under an umbrella of protection. I am also building up my spiritual armor. I will make it all the way, no matter what it feels like today. Faithfulness is the watch word for this prayer.

I receive. I accept. I embrace.

Reflections:

TRUST ACCOUNT

Yesterday, today, and tomorrow, I live and move in the one. Whatever I am feeling at any moment, I know that I am never alone. In my daily living on the earth I know that I will experience ups and downs. I know deeply that my faith must be constant in trusting Spirit. My belief in Spirit means I trust the universal Omnipotent God. I trust in Spirit who is love. I trust in Spirit who is faithful to provide all of my needs, even when I may be disciplined in challenges of daily living. I know that God's desire is to bless, restore, and make me whole.

I receive. I accept. I embrace.

Reflections:

August 30 — GOOD ORDERLY DIRECTION

Yesterday, today, and tomorrow, I live and move in the one. Whatever I am feeling at any moment, I know that I am never alone. I must always remember that faith comes by learning to listen and listening to learn. I also know that faith comes by the still small voice of **G**ood **O**rderly **D**irection, and not by the news, media or social networks.

I receive. I accept. I embrace.

Reflections:

August 31

Yesterday, today, and tomorrow, I live and move in the one. Whatever I am feeling at any moment, I know that I am never alone. I know that what I listen to affects my soul, my heart, and my mind. I turn my ears, heart, and mind to feed my soul in the right way. Depression, recession, and unemployment are not in my plans for God's life.

I receive. I accept. I embrace.

Reflections:

GOOD ORDERLY DIRECTION

SEPTEMBER

Morning Glory

Ayin M. Adams, Ph.D. September 1

Yesterday, today, and tomorrow, I live and move in the one. Whatever I am feeling at any moment, I know that I am never alone. I know that love is the fulfilling of the law. I know that love is my nature.

I receive. I accept. I embrace.

Reflections:
_____
_____
_____
_____
_____
_____

September 2 — **GOOD ORDERLY DIRECTION**

Yesterday, today, and tomorrow, I live and move in the one. Whatever I am feeling at any moment, I know that I am never alone. I know that love is the frequency of energy that creates me, makes me co-creator, and surrounds me no matter where I am. I know that in love there is fulfillment, through love I know myself, and in expressing love, I am one with my world.

I receive. I accept. I embrace.

Reflections:

Yesterday, today, and tomorrow, I live and move in the one. Whatever I am feeling at any moment, I know that I am never alone. What am I willing to nurture this moment? In my heart of hearts, I know that I would nurture a deep desire to grow and a deep need for inner peace. This nurturing would mean a better understanding of myself. This would mean a time of letting go, and a time for communication that I have never known before. I know that in this scared space, no one can touch it. It is me. It is mine. It is now.

I receive. I accept. I embrace.

Reflections:

September 4 **GOOD ORDERLY DIRECTION**

Yesterday, today, and tomorrow, I live and move in the one. Whatever I am feeling at any moment, I know that I am never alone. I am ready and willing to know It, to experience It, and to give It flow, which means: let It come forth.

I know that It is a seed that is ready to open up after its' own kind. I need only ask myself, "Who could nurture it more than my love? Who could embrace it more tenderly than my acceptance? Who could know it more intimately, and who can give way to it? I know that my answer is only me. I can!

I receive. I accept. I embrace.

Reflections:

Ayin M. Adams, Ph.D. September 5

Yesterday, today, and tomorrow, I live and move in the one. Whatever I am feeling at any moment, I know that I am never alone. I know that I am important to the universe, and that the universe chooses this moment to express itself as me. I know that my child-like self says yes. It is an exuberance that dances with joy. It is my inner faith that says I am ready.

I receive. I accept. I embrace.

Reflections:

September 6   **GOOD ORDERLY DIRECTION**

Yesterday, today, and tomorrow, I live and move in the one. Whatever I am feeling at any moment, I know that I am never alone. I know that the light of my own being is saying, "It is a new day, a new dawning, and I am waking up." I know that there is so much energy I cannot contain it in words. I am a conduit. I can do it. I am receptive. I am ready. I am willing. I will to Will the will of God. I allow my whole being to say yes, and this is the beginning of true being- ness. And so it is.

I receive. I accept. I embrace.

Reflections: _____
_____
_____
_____
_____
_____

Yesterday, today, and tomorrow, I live and move in the one. Whatever I am feeling at any moment, I know that I am never alone. I know that whatever is not for my highest good now fades from my consciousness and is released. I no longer desire it. I know right now that Divine Intelligence is opening the way for my immediate blessings. I have faith that all that is mine by Divine right now comes to me in rich abundance. My blessings do not interfere with anyone else's good. God's rich substance is unlimited and everywhere for all to use. It arrives in Divine time. My desires are richly fulfilled in God's own wonderful way.

I receive. I accept. I embrace.

Reflections:

September 8   **GOOD ORDERLY DIRECTION**

SERENITY

Yesterday, today, and tomorrow, I live and move in the one. Whatever I am feeling at any moment, I know that I am never alone. I live in a state of serenity. I know that my life is in balance. I express only the beautiful, the good, and the true. I am fulfilled and content. All things are joyous in my world. I live as God would want me to live: fully expressed with enthusiasm and boundless joy.

I receive. I accept. I embrace.

Reflections:

NEW DAY, NEW BEGINNING

Yesterday, today, and tomorrow, I live and move in the one. Whatever I am feeling at any moment, I know that I am never alone. Each day becomes a fresh new experience when I allow the Divine to unfold within me. I know that this unfoldment takes place in consciousness. I allow the Divine flow to provide exciting new avenues of demonstration to take place in me, through me, and by means of me.

I receive. I accept. I embrace.

Reflections:

September 10   **GOOD ORDERLY DIRECTION**

HARMONY

Yesterday, today, and tomorrow, I live and move in the one. Whatever I am feeling at any moment, I know that I am never alone. No longer am I confused by world conditions. I am not confused by the opinions of others. I am certain within myself of my own perfect good. I am certain that I am in harmony and at peace with myself, the world, and everyone in it. Today, I accept myself as harmony. I am this harmony.

I receive. I accept. I embrace.

Reflections:

September 11

Yesterday, today, and tomorrow, I live and move in the one. Whatever I am feeling at any moment, I know that I am never alone. I know that I am one with Divine Order. I know that I am in harmony with the cosmos. The Infinite created this cosmos in order and in harmony. I know that Divine Order and harmony exists in my soul.

I receive. I accept. I embrace.

Reflections:

September 12   **GOOD ORDERLY DIRECTION**

Yesterday, today, and tomorrow, I live and move in the one. Whatever I am feeling at any moment, I know that I am never alone. As a result all is at ease. There is no strain. There is no tension, because all is in Divine Order, harmony, and peace. I am relaxed. I proceed with the business of living because I am the harmony of truth made manifest. And so it is.

I receive. I accept. I embrace.

Reflections:
___
___
___
___
___

RESPONSIBILITY

Yesterday, today, and tomorrow, I live and move in the one. Whatever I am feeling at any moment, I know that I am never alone. I know that there are opportunities available to me that allow me to become more fully awake, more fully alert, and more fully aware. When I make my choices in each and every moment I know that I am a Divine being of love taking responsibility.

I receive. I accept. I embrace.

Reflections:

September 14   **GOOD ORDERLY DIRECTION**

Yesterday, today, and tomorrow, I live and move in the one. Whatever I am feeling at any moment, I know that I am never alone. No longer do I cast negative predictions based on hopes and fears. No longer do I focus on what is going to happen later. I now move more fully into the present moment. I now make conscious choices for my thoughts, my feelings, and my actions. I am responsible.

I receive. I accept. I embrace.

Reflections:

September 15

Yesterday, today, and tomorrow, I live and move in the one. Whatever I am feeling at any moment, I know that I am never alone. I encourage myself to take responsibility for every feeling I have. I know that by taking responsibility for my feelings I can see where my feelings take me. I know that this (seeing) leads directly to my thought patterns. When I do this I know that it shows up in my belief that holds me in a prison and reveals the illusion. I take responsibility for my thoughts.

I receive. I accept. I embrace.

Reflections:

September 16 — **GOOD ORDERLY DIRECTION**

RELAXATION

Yesterday, today, and tomorrow, I live and move in the one. Whatever I am feeling at any moment, I know that I am never alone. I must be patient with myself and remember to give myself a loving pat on the back (for the good that I know and do). I know that I have all eternity to achieve my goal. As long as I continue to work and keep patient with myself and others I will succeed.

I receive. I accept. I embrace.

Reflections:

Yesterday, today, and tomorrow, I live and move in the one. Whatever I am feeling at any moment, I know that I am never alone. I know that it is not the problem of time but the way I deal with time. The question is do I have room for a change of pace and relaxation? I need to take time and 'make time' for relaxation and a change of pace. I must make time; otherwise I'll talk myself out of it.

I receive. I accept. I embrace.

Reflections:

September 18 — **GOOD ORDERLY DIRECTION**

Yesterday, today, and tomorrow, I live and move in the one. Whatever I am feeling at any moment, I know that I am never alone. I can have a marvelous relaxation in just five minutes, or I can remain filled with pressure during long hours even when doing nothing. If I keep consciously centered within myself I can keep up a busy schedule. I can carry heavy loads and produce great amounts of work without any pressure at all. There is always a center of repose within the arena of work. I can depend on the inner guidance to make decisions. I can trust the process to evolve with creative ideas and unfoldment. I can truly cast my burdens on the law, Spiritual law. Truly he that is within me is always greater than he that is in the world.

I receive. I accept. I embrace.

Reflections:

OUTGROWING FORM

Yesterday, today, and tomorrow, I live and move in the one. Whatever I am feeling at any moment, I know that I am never alone. I know that this is a time of loss. I know that the life I have lived has outgrown its form. I have been watching and reviewing during the past decade. My work has come full circle. I have outgrown my old form. I do not resist. I know that my old form must die so that new energy can be released into my new form. I prepare for a loss of someone or something that I have had an emotional bond with. I know that this old way of life is coming to a close. I have outgrown it. This is a big change for me.

I receive. I accept. I embrace.

Reflections: _____
_____
_____
_____
_____
_____

September 20   **GOOD ORDERLY DIRECTION**

GRACE

Yesterday, today, and tomorrow, I live and move in the one. Whatever I am feeling at any moment, I know that I am never alone. No longer am I content with being right. I am grace in action. I know that as a servant of God, I must be gentle. I must serve in a gentle capacity. I am grace in action.

I receive. I accept. I embrace.

Reflections: _____
_____
_____
_____
_____
_____

Yesterday, today, and tomorrow, I live and move in the one. Whatever I am feeling at any moment, I know that I am never alone. I know that every step of grace must be preceded by understanding it in a prayerful way, and then making a firm decision to receive it. I know that I will embrace it. Every time my heart beats, my cells are re-programmed in that moment. I become what I believe I am in that moment. I am grace.

I receive. I accept. I embrace.

Reflections:

September 22   **GOOD ORDERLY DIRECTION**

Yesterday, today, and tomorrow, I live and move in the one. Whatever I am feeling at any moment, I know that I am never alone. No longer do I argue with others. As a servant of God I must not argue, curse, fuss, or fight. Instead I must be kind to everyone so that I am able to teach them. I must not hold onto resentments. If I have resentment, this means that I am holding a bat over one's head to beat them up with it. But really, I am beating up myself, because on a spiritual level, there is only one person present and that is me. I am grace in action.

I receive. I accept. I embrace.

Reflections: _____
_____
_____
_____
_____

Yesterday, today, and tomorrow, I live and move in the one. Whatever I am feeling at any moment, I know that I am never alone. Anyone who is in disharmony or conflict with me, I must gently teach. I know that God will heal one's negative thoughts about me. This leads one's mind into a true understanding of another and a feeling of true sisterhood/brotherhood. I know that one will come to his/her senses and break from a mindset which leads to despair. This is true grace.

I receive. I accept. I embrace.

Reflections:

September 24 — **GOOD ORDERLY DIRECTION**

FULL PARTNERSHIP

Yesterday, today, and tomorrow, I live and move in the one. Whatever I am feeling at any moment, I know that I am never alone. There is a line in the song that goes, "Everything must change." There is a powerful force of change at work in my life. There has been change in work, play, and letting go. This change in letting go includes identification and renewal of my spirit. I feel extremely light. I know that what I seek is now seeking me. I welcome the challenge of a full partnership. I am ready. I welcome a partnership in which both of us are on the same level: emotionally, mentally, spiritually, and physically. I know that this change is considered a challenge because it is new. This partnership brings much freedom. I welcome this partnership which is equal and respectful. I recognize and realize this as such. I know that my partner is balanced. No one comes to me to be fixed. Each one of us is balanced and can stand in our own truth.

I receive. I accept. I embrace.

Reflections:

Yesterday, today, and tomorrow, I live and move in the one. Whatever I am feeling at any moment, I know that I am never alone. I must be honest and take healthy right action when I notice that the relationship is on a fast moving train going straight to hell. It is going nowhere good. I must be authentic with myself; no longer do I waste time and energy foolishly. This is not my drama. I get myself together.

I receive. I accept. I embrace.

Reflections:

September 26   **GOOD ORDERLY DIRECTION**

Yesterday, today, and tomorrow, I live and move in the one. Whatever I am feeling at any moment, I know that I am never alone. It is easy to be pulled into another's entanglements and drama. If there is a tendency to pull me into drama, I must be cautious. I know that people want to live a certain way but will continue using old selfish ways to manipulate others. I do not allow another's feelings to be transpose onto my feelings. I stand far away from this type of energy and I do not get close. Often, a person may be living the best life that is possible with whatever tools are available. I use caution. I must allow each person the opportunity to pull his/herself up by his/her own boot straps. I am not another's crutch. I use discernment wisely.

I receive. I accept. I embrace.

Reflections:

Yesterday, today, and tomorrow, I live and move in the one. Whatever I am feeling at any moment, I know that I am never alone. I know that I must avoid feeding my soul garbage. I kick fear to the curb. I feed myself with the fruits of the Spirit: love, joy, truth, compassion, and faith. I let my life become a manifestation to receive the supernatural blessings from God.

I receive. I accept. I embrace.

Reflections:

September 28   **GOOD ORDERLY DIRECTION**

Yesterday, today, and tomorrow, I live and move in the one. Whatever I am feeling at any moment, I know that I am never alone. As a spiritual newborn baby, I ask Spirit to show me how to build up my armor and make my faith strong. Today, being faithful and trusting, I went to the bank and made a deposit to God. I know that God is always loyal to me. I know that I have a spiritual bank account with God who will always take care of me. I can withdraw and receive my needs and wants.

I receive. I accept. I embrace.

Reflections:

Yesterday, today, and tomorrow, I live and move in the one. Whatever I am feeling at any moment, I know that I am never alone. I refrain from entering into relationships that I have to constantly fix. It is too much work. I know that a healthy relationship is not a person always wanting to take something from me, whether it is public image or notoriety. I avoid the trap and tread carefully. I desire a partner who I do not have to fix. I use spiritual discernment. When my authentic partner arrives, I will know. There will be no fixing, or helping, or asking, "What happened to you when you were ten?" There is no story. There will be no agenda.

I receive. I accept. I embrace.

Reflections:

PAIN

Yesterday, today, and tomorrow, I live and move in the one. Whatever I am feeling at any moment, I know that I am never alone. Whenever I am experiencing pain or suffering, I know that I am undergoing a passage into the light. I control anger and restrain impulses during these times. I keep my faith firm. I learn to wait upon the will of Heaven. I know that that my joy is coming. I know that light is coming. I know that new clarity, full restoration, and self alignment are coming. Indeed, the power and will of Heaven is here now, available to me in this moment to conquer pain.

I receive. I accept. I embrace.

Reflections:

Ayin M. Adams, Ph.D.

GOOD ORDERLY DIRECTION

OCTOBER

Yellow Calendula

Yesterday, today, and tomorrow, I live and move in the one. Whatever I am feeling at any moment, I know that I am never alone. I walk tall in confidence, and I walk softly and quietly upon the earth.

I receive. I accept. I embrace.

Reflections:

October 2 — **GOOD ORDERLY DIRECTION**

MINDING MY OWN BUSINESS

Yesterday, today, and tomorrow, I live and move in the one. Whatever I am feeling at any moment, I know that I am never alone. I interjected myself into your life without your asking me. I robbed you of your own opportunity. I know that you are learning and growing for yourself. I do not need to be in your life, even if I have the best of intentions. Please forgive me.

I receive. I accept. I embrace.

Reflections:

Yesterday, today, and tomorrow, I live and move in the one. Whatever I am feeling at any moment, I know that I am never alone. I know that I do not need to stick my nose into your business especially if you did not ask for it, nor call me for help. I am learning to know when and how to make comments. I am staying in my lane. I release you and focus on myself and what I need to be doing. May God bless you.

I receive. I accept. I embrace.

Reflections:

October 4 — **GOOD ORDERLY DIRECTION**

PROSPERITY

Yesterday, today, and tomorrow, I live and move in the one. Whatever I am feeling at any moment, I know that I am never alone. I claim my Divine birthright of health, wealth, and happiness. No longer do I depend on another person, on property, or on status to supply my needs. I depend absolutely on the love of God. This is true goodness. I claim my good.

I receive. I accept. I embrace.

Reflections:

Yesterday, today, and tomorrow, I live and move in the one. Whatever I am feeling at any moment, I know that I am never alone. Money is not my supply. No person, place, or thing is my supply. Spirit is my supply.

I receive. I accept. I embrace.

Reflections:

October 6 — **GOOD ORDERLY DIRECTION**

Yesterday, today, and tomorrow, I live and move in the one. Whatever I am feeling at any moment, I know that I am never alone. I am fully aware and conscious of Spirit as my abundance. I am fully aware and conscious of Spirit is constant activity of Infinite prosperity in my life.

I receive. I accept. I embrace.

Reflections: _____
_____
_____
_____
_____
_____

Yesterday, today, and tomorrow, I live and move in the one. Whatever I am feeling at any moment, I know that I am never alone. I open my mind to a greater understanding of my relationship to the Creator, and of my life to greater use in service. I open my hands to receive the showers of blessings that the Creator's hands are always holding out to me.

I receive. I accept. I embrace.

Reflections:

October 8 — **GOOD ORDERLY DIRECTION**

Yesterday, today, and tomorrow, I live and move in the one. Whatever I am feeling at any moment, I know that I am never alone. I open every avenue of my being to permit the richness of the Creator's love to enter. I am God's beloved child in whom God is well pleased. I open every avenue of my being to permit God's richness to bless me.

I receive. I accept. I embrace.

Reflections:

Yesterday, today, and tomorrow, I live and move in the one. Whatever I am feeling at any moment, I know that I am never alone. I open my pocketbook and bank account to the inflowing stream of God's rich substance. Money is a manifest form of the invisible substances in which God has clothed his creation. Money flows to me and out from me in every direction as God directs it.

I receive. I accept. I embrace.

Reflections:

October 10 — **GOOD ORDERLY DIRECTION**

Yesterday, today, and tomorrow, I live and move in the one. Whatever I am feeling at any moment, I know that I am never alone. I am an open channel for the inflow and the outflow of God's love. I owe no man or woman anything but love. The law of love has filled my treasure chest to overflow.

I receive. I accept. I embrace.

Reflections:

Yesterday, today, and tomorrow, I live and move in the one. Whatever I am feeling at any moment, I know that I am never alone. My obligation is to the Creator for the continued unlimited good that flows to and through me. I fulfill these obligations by keeping the high watch and continuing to be steadfast in faith. I recognize the good in everything and in everyone. I recognize, realize, and accept only the good. There is good to spare and good to share.

I receive. I accept. I embrace.

Reflections:

October 12 — **GOOD ORDERLY DIRECTION**

Yesterday, today, and tomorrow, I live and move in the one. Whatever I am feeling at any moment, I know that I am never alone. I do not believe in losses. I live, move, and have my being in Spirit which can suffer no loss.

I receive. I accept. I embrace.

Reflections:

Yesterday, today, and tomorrow, I live and move in the one. Whatever I am feeling at any moment, I know that I am never alone. There is no lack in my life. I lift my vision above the material realm to the spiritual realm. The law of love has enabled me to pay my debts and have forgiven all debts owed to me.

I receive. I accept. I embrace.

Reflections:

October 14 — **GOOD ORDERLY DIRECTION**

Yesterday, today, and tomorrow, I live and move in the one. Whatever I am feeling at any moment, I know that I am never alone. I abide in the glory of God's presence, richness beyond comprehension until my human mind is saturated with the Divine Mind.

I receive. I accept. I embrace.

Reflections: _____
_____
_____
_____
_____

Ayin M. Adams, Ph.D. October 15

Yesterday, today, and tomorrow, I live and move in the one. Whatever I am feeling at any moment, I know that I am never alone. Beloved Creator, I know that you have fulfilled the covenant and multiply the good on my path until all the sorrow and until all the sadness have flown away. Holy One, I have entered into a place of everlasting gladness.

I receive. I accept. I embrace.

Reflections: _____
_____
_____
_____
_____
_____

October 16 — **GOOD ORDERLY DIRECTION**

Yesterday, today, and tomorrow, I live and move in the one. Whatever I am feeling at any moment, I know that I am never alone. I know that as I walk and talk with God in the garden of my soul, I am released from all thought and labor. I know that you have given me the power to speak of your invisible substance so that it manifest in my world according to my spoken word.

I receive. I accept. I embrace.

Reflections:

Yesterday, today, and tomorrow, I live and move in the one. Whatever I am feeling at any moment, I know that I am never alone. I know that everything and everyone in my world is enriched because of my companionship with Spirit. I know that every act of my life has become a joyous service of love to Spirit, and to my fellow human beings. Throughout eternity I shall be thine and thou shall be mine.

I receive. I accept. I embrace.

Reflections:

October 18   **GOOD ORDERLY DIRECTION**

Yesterday, today, and tomorrow, I live and move in the one. Whatever I am feeling at any moment, I know that I am never alone. I give thanks to the Creator, Father-Mother God-Goddess. In this inner richness I abide, and in this glory I am truly blessed. And so it is.

I receive. I accept. I embrace.

Reflections:

Yesterday, today, and tomorrow, I live and move in the one. Whatever I am feeling at any moment, I know that I am never alone. I am a rich child of a loving Creator. All that the Creator has is mine to share and to experience. Divine Intelligence is now showing me how to claim my own God-given wealth, health, and happiness.

I receive. I accept. I embrace.

Reflections:

RELATIONSHIPS: LONLINESS

Yesterday, today, and tomorrow, I live and move in the one. Whatever I am feeling at any moment, I know that I am never alone. I know that one of the great problems of life either for those who have been through an unhappy marriage or those who are unhappily unmarried, is the desperate experience of loneliness, and the desire to form a fulfilling relationship. I know that there is a common belief that when one finds the right person their loneliness will be over and their life will be full and fulfilled. If they just find that right person; Mr. Right or Ms. Right. Loneliness is not just being alone, it is completely psychological, it is a deficiency of the Spirit. It can only be corrected when one overcomes that deficiency. Loneliness comes not because one has not found the right friends, but because one has not found one's self. Before one can do much about forming a relationship with another person one must first of all form a good relationship with oneself.

I receive. I accept. I embrace.

Reflections:

BRODER SPIRITUAL VISION

Yesterday, today, and tomorrow, I live and move in the one. Whatever I am feeling at any moment, I know that I am never alone. I see through eyes of love. I see through spiritual vision. I have been given more wisdom, more vision, more help, and a wider scope. I have been given more spiritual tools to work with. I have help. I am not alone. I am the one enjoying the flight of the eagle flying free from entanglements to see a broader vision. I now see and understand more. I have a bird's eye view. And if I am lifted up, I will draw others unto me.

I receive. I accept. I embrace.

Reflections:

October 22   **GOOD ORDERLY DIRECTION**

Yesterday, today, and tomorrow, I live and move in the one. Whatever I am feeling at any moment, I know that I am never alone. I know that I have been brought forth by Spirit and made to live in a larger palace within. I know that Spirit delights in me. I delight in Spirit to do the will of good. My true destiny is being fulfilled; I and the Father are one. God's thoughts are my thoughts. God's actions are my actions.

I receive. I accept. I embrace.

Reflections: _____
_____
_____
_____
_____
_____

GOD

Yesterday, today, and tomorrow, I live and move in the one. Whatever I am feeling at any moment, I know that I am never alone. No longer do I have problems using the name GOD. I know that God is:

Good

Orderly

Direction

When I follow good orderly directions I receive positive and healthy results manifested in my life as a consequence of trusting the loving process as it unfolds.

I receive. I accept. I embrace.

Reflections:

October 24   **GOOD ORDERLY DIRECTION**

Yesterday, today, and tomorrow, I live and move in the one. Whatever I am feeling at any moment, I know that I am never alone. I lift my eyes towards the Divine and I am shown glimpses of Heaven. I have seen and touched the love of God. I hear God even in bird song.

I receive. I accept. I embrace.

Reflections: _____
_____
_____
_____
_____
_____

Yesterday, today, and tomorrow, I live and move in the one. Whatever I am feeling at any moment, I know that I am never alone. I know that there are temptations, trials, and tribulations in the world. I know that God is faithful and will not test me to be tempted above which I am able, but with the temptation provide a way of escape, that I may be able to bear it.

I receive. I accept. I embrace.

Reflections:

October 26   **GOOD ORDERLY DIRECTION**

INTIMACY

Yesterday, today, and tomorrow, I live and move in the one. Whatever I am feeling at any moment, I know that I am never alone. I know that intimacy first occurs and belongs to self. I owe it to myself to understand myself. What do I see about myself that I can confidently share with another? Intimacy is: In
>
>   To
>
>   Me
>
>   I
>
>   See.

This is a most sacred and holy act of sharing myself intimately.

I receive. I accept. I embrace.

Reflections: _____
_____
_____
_____
_____

Yesterday, today, and tomorrow, I live and move in the one. Whatever I am feeling at any moment, I know that I am never alone. It is important that I develop my intimacy with Spirit. I want to share such an intimacy. I have the knowing that Spirit has my back and will not let me down. The more intimacy I have, the easier it is to receive thoughts from Spirit.

I receive. I accept. I embrace.

Reflections:

October 28 — GOOD ORDERLY DIRECTION

Yesterday, today, and tomorrow, I live and move in the one. Whatever I am feeling at any moment, I know that I am never alone. I developed this intimacy by hearing, reading powerful metaphysical thoughts, and listening to Spirit. This intimacy drops into my spirit and a deeper wisdom comes. Next, my spirit and God's spirit becomes One. I am then led and directed where to step, where to look, where to go, to make this move, or to not make a move. I get help. Abundance comes to me in wealth, people, and situations. I am like the flying eagle soaring free from entanglements, lifting and rising above the flow of ordinary life to acquire a broader vision.

I receive. I accept. I embrace.

Reflections: _____
_____
_____
_____
_____
_____

TRUSTING TEST

Yesterday, today, and tomorrow, I live and move in the one. Whatever I am feeling at any moment, I know that I am never alone. When joy eludes me I know that I must stay firm and in a tranquil state. There is no need to get my feathers ruffled. Today I stand my ground for patience, clarity, and perseverance. Everything is a test.

I receive. I accept. I embrace.

Reflections: _____
_____
_____
_____
_____
_____

October 30 — **GOOD ORDERLY DIRECTION**

SPIRITUAL CPR

Yesterday, today, and tomorrow, I live and move in the one. Whatever I am feeling at any moment, I know that I am never alone. I know that without ears to hear and eyes to see I may fail to take advantage of the moment. This could well lead to an opportunity missed or a weakening of my position. Right now minor failures and disappointments may pass by unconsciously unaware. I know that for everything I experience there is a beginning, middle, and an end, and is followed by a new beginning. Therefore I do not draw back from the passage into darkness. When in deep waters I become a diver.

I receive. I accept. I embrace.

Reflections: _____
_____
_____
_____
_____
_____

Winter of Life

Yesterday, today, and tomorrow, I live and move in the one. Whatever I am feeling at any moment, I know that I am never alone. When the winter of life is upon me this means that I am upon a winter of spiritual life; of coldness and chill. During this time I must be patient. I know that this is the period of gestation that precedes my rebirth. This freeze leads me to trusting Spirit. During this time, I let go of what I am holding onto. I let go of the fear. I let go to bring release. I let go of the mistrust, and let God lead me. I let go of anxiety, and I let go of negative feelings. I surrender all to Spirit and I display wisdom and courage in the midst of trusting. I remain mindful that the seed has been planted and is present in me. I water the seed with faithfulness as part of my rebirth.

I receive. I accept. I embrace.

Reflections:

GOOD ORDERLY DIRECTION

NOVEMBER

Red Chrysanthemum

Yesterday, today, and tomorrow, I live and move in the one. Whatever I am feeling at any moment, I know that I am never alone. I suit up, I show up, and I follow through, knowing that Divine Intelligence is at work in my life and in my affairs.

I receive. I accept. I embrace.

Reflections:

November 2 **GOOD ORDERLY DIRECTION**

Yesterday, today and tomorrow, I live and move in the one, whatever I am feeling at any moment I know that I am never alone. I am never a victim of circumstance. I am never a creature of chance. My life is lived from within out. I claim victory over any odds and difficulties in my life.

I receive. I accept. I embrace.

Reflections:

Yesterday, today, and tomorrow, I live and move in the one. Whatever I am feeling at any moment, I know that I am never alone. I know that everything truly is in Divine Order, in spite of appearances. I trust this truth.

I receive. I accept. I embrace.

Reflections: _____
_____
_____
_____
_____
_____

November 4   **GOOD ORDERLY DIRECTION**

Yesterday, today, and tomorrow, I live and move in the one. Whatever I am feeling at any moment, I know that I am never alone. I know that what I resist only persists until I turn frustration into a true celebration.

I receive. I accept. I embrace.

Reflections:

CONTROLLING EMOTIONS

Yesterday, today, and tomorrow, I live and move in the one. Whatever I am feeling at any moment, I know that I am never alone. I have emotions, but I am not my emotions. I have feelings, but I am not my feelings. I am the master of my domain.

I receive. I accept. I embrace.

Reflections:

November 6 — GOOD ORDERLY DIRECTION

Yesterday, today, and tomorrow, I live and move in the one. Whatever I am feeling at any moment, I know that I am never alone. I live in gratitude. I know that gratitude is an attitude. I am here to give and to demonstrate who I am. I am perfect just the way I am. I am grateful.

I receive. I accept. I embrace.

Reflections:

Ayin M. Adams, Ph.D. November 7

Yesterday, today, and tomorrow, I live and move in the one. Whatever I am feeling at any moment, I know that I am never alone. The purpose of my life is to be who I am. I am the light. I express my light. I demonstrate my light.

I receive. I accept. I embrace.

Reflections: _____
_____
_____
_____
_____
_____

November 8 — **GOOD ORDERLY DIRECTION**

Yesterday, today, and tomorrow, I live and move in the one. Whatever I am feeling at any moment, I know that I am never alone. I know that I always do have a choice. I know that no matter what looms before me or what lies behind me or what is present around me, I can still think great thoughts or small thoughts. How I think becomes what manifests in my life. It also determines what I become, great or small. Thankfulness makes me great. I know that without this spirit of gratitude and thankfulness, I may become a little person with a little mind, leading a little and inconsequential life.

I receive. I accept. I embrace.

Reflections:

Yesterday, today, and tomorrow, I live and move in the one. Whatever I am feeling at any moment, I know that I am never alone. I remember those moments when things have not gone well, when I have experienced failures, reverses, and difficulties. I have asked the question, "How can I voice gratitude at such times without being hypocritical or dishonest?" I know that during these times I was not thanking God for what was on my table or what was in my bank account, because it was very meager indeed. I was thankful for what was in my heart. I know that it was a conscious choice to turn from darkness to light, from lack to abundance, to look up beyond the appearances, and beyond the prosaic. And this looking up was preparing the way for the many blessings and the very consciousness that I hold today.

I receive. I accept. I embrace.

Reflections: _____
_____
_____
_____
_____
_____

November 10   **GOOD ORDERLY DIRECTION**

Yesterday, today and tomorrow, I live and move in the one. Whatever I am feeling at any moment, I know that I am never alone. I know that the need to be kind raises the consciousness of one who is kind and the one who is receiving kindness.

I receive. I accept. I embrace.

Reflections:
___

GRATITUDE

Yesterday, today, and tomorrow, I live and move in the one. Whatever I am feeling at any moment, I know that I am never alone. I know that gratitude is not just a virtue for which I am given points. Gratitude is an attitude that lifts me to the highest level of consciousness and enables me to experience the highest kind of life.

I receive. I accept. I embrace.

Reflections: _____
_____
_____
_____
_____
_____

November 12   **GOOD ORDERLY DIRECTION**

Yesterday, today, and tomorrow, I live and move in the one. Whatever I am feeling at any moment, I know that I am never alone. Plato says, "A grateful mind is a great mind which will eventually attract to itself great things." I know that a grateful person is great because he/she has turned on the lights within. I do not really need to have things for which to be grateful. But, when I give thanks, I radiate a light by which I see many things for which I am grateful. In addition, I tend to attract things to me for which I can be grateful.

I receive. I accept. I embrace.

Reflections: _____
_____
_____
_____
_____
_____

Yesterday, today, and tomorrow, I live and move in the one. Whatever I am feeling at any moment, I know that I am never alone. I claim my health and wholeness. When my mind is at ease, then I know that dis-ease will disappear. I know that disease is wrong thinking.

I receive. I accept. I embrace.

Reflections:

November 14   **GOOD ORDERLY DIRECTION**

Yesterday, today and tomorrow, I live and move in the one, whatever I am feeling at any moment I know that I am never alone. My growth in relationships and myself will commence when I discover and learn the depths in myself and my partner. I know that this is when my true relationship will begin.

I receive. I accept. I embrace.

Reflections:

Ayin M. Adams, Ph.D. November 15

Yesterday, today and tomorrow, I live and move in the one, whatever I am feeling at any moment I know that I am never alone. When I am feeling overwhelmed and exhausted, I must keep my faith firm. The school of suffering will graduate a rare scholar. What is mine will come to me; I must believe this.

I receive. I accept. I embrace.

Reflections:

November 16   **GOOD ORDERLY DIRECTION**

ALL THINGS ARE POSSIBLE

Yesterday, today, and tomorrow, I live and move in the one. Whatever I am feeling at any moment, I know that I am never alone. I know that thanksgiving is a kind of mind opener which opens the flow of the Divine process to us. I recall Emily Cady's words in Lessons in Truth, "There's something about the mental act of thanksgiving that seems to carry the human mind far beyond the region of doubt into the clear atmosphere of faith and trust where all things are possible."

I receive. I accept. I embrace.

Reflections:

Ayin M. Adams, Ph.D. November 17

Yesterday, today, and tomorrow, I live and move in the one. Whatever I am feeling at any moment, I know that I am never alone. If your heart is heavy at this moment weighed down by disappointment, fear, or grief, the idea of giving thanks may seem useless, impossible, or as I said earlier, even hypocritical and dishonest. How can you be thankful when you have lost your job? How can you give thanks when you business is failing? How can you experience a true thanksgiving when your heart is aching over the loss of a loved one, or someone who has run away? I know that it is difficult to get into a true sincere consciousness of thanksgiving.

I receive. I accept. I embrace.

Reflections:

November 18   **GOOD ORDERLY DIRECTION**

Yesterday, today, and tomorrow, I live and move in the one. Whatever I am feeling at any moment, I know that I am never alone. I know that if I still my mind and give thanks for my challenges, give thanks for my difficulties, my hurts, my disappointments, and my betrayals, I know that if I turn it inside out I'll find God there. Then I will find that my problem is a blessing in disguise.

I receive. I accept. I embrace.

Reflections:

Yesterday, today, and tomorrow, I live and move in the one. Whatever I am feeling at any moment, I know that I am never alone. The Chinese says crisis is danger plus opportunity. I know that crisis is a difficulty. It also presents an opportunity to grow and an opportunity to change. I know that this will be a great turning point in my life and a very beautiful experience. I will always remember the words that rise up in my stillness, "Give thanks, give thanks for it."

I receive. I accept. I embrace.

Reflections: _____
_____
_____
_____
_____
_____

November 20 **GOOD ORDERLY DIRECTION**

Yesterday, today, and tomorrow, I live and move in the one. Whatever I am feeling at any moment, I know that I am never alone. I know that whatever may be the difficulty that I am facing right now, I just need to give thanks for it. I will give thanks that somehow in the experience, in the crisis, in the challenge, in the difficulty, in the change, there will be a turning point that will lead me into some new experience, new growth, new unfoldment, new development, and new blessings that ultimately will put me in a point where I can look back and say, "Well, difficult as it was it was a very important moment in my life."

I receive. I accept. I embrace.

Reflections:

Ayin M. Adams, Ph.D.   November 21

Yesterday, today, and tomorrow, I live and move in the one. Whatever I am feeling at any moment, I know that I am never alone. In an attitude of gratitude I will take time today to sift through the sands of my life and set down the things for which I can give thanks. I must not settle for the obvious. I give thanks for my hungers, my longings, my yearnings, and for the unfolding good that they have revealed.

I receive. I accept. I embrace.

Reflections:

November 22 **GOOD ORDERLY DIRECTION**

Yesterday, today, and tomorrow, I live and move in the one. Whatever I am feeling at any moment, I know that I am never alone. I know that I will give thanks for the people in my life and for the good they have revealed or that which my perception is learning to see. I know that I will give thanks that I am alive and living in a world that has such excitement, challenge, change, and even difficulty.

I receive. I accept. I embrace.

Reflections: _____
_____
_____
_____
_____
_____

Yesterday, today, and tomorrow, I live and move in the one. Whatever I am feeling at any moment, I know that I am never alone. There is an inner sanctuary within me. It is the gateway to the otherworld. I have glimpsed into the other world. I know that I have special power. I know that there are powerful changes at work in my life that are of a secret sacred manner. There is a profound secret coming to me through the Yew Tree. There is a deep probing of meaning, profit, and gain in my life. I know that the Yew Tree holds magical mystical powers for me.

I receive. I accept. I embrace.

Reflections:

November 24 **GOOD ORDERLY DIRECTION**

Yesterday, today, and tomorrow, I live and move in the one. Whatever I am feeling at any moment, I know that I am never alone. I know that I take on great causes. I also know that I nurture people. I am a humanitarian. It is in my contract with God to get the job done. I remain in love. I remain in humility.

I receive. I accept. I embrace.

Reflections:

Ayin M. Adams, Ph.D. November 25

Yesterday, today, and tomorrow, I live and move in the one. Whatever I am feeling at any moment, I know that I am never alone. When I am searching for a sense of peace with my soul, I bring harmony in my total awareness. I recognize and realize my union with all life, with Oneness. I know that I am safe. I know that I will be taken care of. I know that I am loved. I know that I have been given the key. I know that I am the key. I know that I am experiencing a 100% partnership.

I receive. I accept. I embrace.

Reflections:

November 26   **GOOD ORDERLY DIRECTION**

EMBRACING DIVINITY OF SELF

Yesterday, today, and tomorrow, I live and move in the one. Whatever I am feeling at any moment, I know that I am never alone. I _____ have been given the key. What do I truly want in my life? _____.

I receive. I accept. I embrace.

Reflections: _____
_____
_____
_____
_____
_____

Yesterday, today, and tomorrow, I live and move in the one. Whatever I am feeling at any moment, I know that I am never alone. I give thanks for the world in which I live. I know that it is a changing world, but so it has always been. I know that there are many cross currents in the world. Man and the civilization that he built, is evolving, growing, developing, and changing. I look up to the stars and see the new ideas and aspirations that are gripping the consciousness of the planet. I believe that they can be achieved in harmony and in love. This is your Thanksgiving Day and I want to give you my very special blessing this day for a happy, wonder- filled Thanksgiving. God bless you.

I receive. I accept. I embrace.

Reflections:

November 28   **GOOD ORDERLY DIRECTION**

Yesterday, today, and tomorrow, I live and move in the one. Whatever I am feeling at any moment, I know that I am never alone. I know that everything returns. I know that patience is needed for the fruit to ripen. I am waiting upon the will of Heaven. I am shown glimpses of the gateway. I conserve what I have already gained. There is no need for excessive striving. I need not push beyond. The powerful forces of change are at work and it is a secret matter. It is between me and the other world. So be it, and so it is!

I receive. I accept. I embrace.

Reflections:

Yesterday, today, and tomorrow, I live and move in the one. Whatever I am feeling at any moment, I know that I am never alone. I know that in order for me to be authentic with myself I must look deeply and honestly into my own heart to discover my level of commitment to my partner's well- being. I must be tuned in to my beloved's relationship to his/her own life, not just narrowly concerned with the relationship to my life.

I receive. I accept. I embrace.

Reflections:

November 30 — **GOOD ORDERLY DIRECTION**

PERSEVERANCE

Yesterday, today, and tomorrow, I live and move in the one. Whatever I am feeling at any moment, I know that I am never alone. I know that true tranquility for me is patience, clarity, and perseverance. I know that everything is a test. Perseverance is the basis for patience, seeing-rightly, and following through.

I receive. I accept. I embrace.

Reflections: _____
_____
_____
_____
_____
_____

Ayin M. Adams, Ph.D.

GOOD ORDERLY DIRECTION

DECEMBER

Holly

Ayin M. Adams, Ph.D. December 1

Yesterday, today, and tomorrow, I live and move in the one. Whatever I am feeling at any moment, I know that I am never alone. Lovers who meet during low periods in their life, and cling to one another for security can only invite a hostage situation which may lead to selfish survival instead of emotional and spiritual growth. One certainly can miss the signs along the highway of life in a sacred manner when it is time to need self. Always remain authentic by cleaning up the wreckage of one's past before engaging in relationships.

I receive. I accept. I embrace.

Reflections: _____
_____
_____
_____
_____
_____

December 2   **GOOD ORDERLY DIRECTION**

Yesterday, today, and tomorrow, I live and move in the one. Whatever I am feeling at any moment, I know that I am never alone. I know that I am free to be me. I dig deeper within my soul where unconditional love and wisdom already exist. I draw upon this inexhaustible source. I am strengthened, nourished, and uplifted. I am worthwhile. I am the most important person in my world to me. Today, I count and I come first and foremost.

I receive. I accept. I embrace.

Reflections: _____
_____
_____
_____
_____
_____

Ayin M. Adams, Ph.D. December 3

Yesterday, today, and tomorrow, I live and move in the one. Whatever I am feeling at any moment, I know that I am never alone. I know that I am deserving of great good and joyous abundant living. I think clearly. I focus on my Oneness with universal love. I accept this clear correct knowing with all my heart. I know that as I now take right action, I bring the words and the love together by doing, by revealing, and by giving. All is made manifest. I am harmonious in all areas of my life.

I receive. I accept. I embrace.

Reflections:

December 4   **GOOD ORDERLY DIRECTION**

Yesterday, today, and tomorrow, I live and move in the one. Whatever I am feeling at any moment, I know that I am never alone. I forgive all persons, places, things, and institutions for any harm done to me, real or imagined. I forgive in order to release the blockages in my life that have held me back from experiencing joy and fulfillment that were meant for me. I now know that there is only love between us.

I receive. I accept. I embrace.

Reflections:

Yesterday, today, and tomorrow, I live and move in the one. Whatever I am feeling at any moment, I know that I am never alone. I forgive myself and I ask you to forgive me for anything I may have ever done to you that caused you pain or sorrow. May there be only love between us. I know that when I take responsibility for healing myself, I will heal, and everyone around me will heal.

I receive. I accept. I embrace.

Reflections:

December 6 — **GOOD ORDERLY DIRECTION**

Yesterday, today, and tomorrow, I live and move in the one. Whatever I am feeling at any moment, I know that I am never alone. I forgive myself and I forgive you totally and unconditionally. I forgive your actions towards me. I know that your actions have made me stronger. I now know that through the healing powers of forgiveness, I am growing spiritually, physically, mentally, and financially. I know that by forgiving you I am loving, caring, giving, successful, and prosperous.

I receive. I accept. I embrace.

Reflections:

INNER GLOW

Yesterday, today, and tomorrow, I live and move in the one. Whatever I am feeling at any moment, I know that I am never alone. No longer am I content with looking outside for my inner glow. I know that all the things that I do in the outer are symbolic. I know that it is what happens within me. I know that it is the inner glow, the inner experience of giving birth to my new awareness, my own Divinity.

I receive. I accept. I embrace.

Reflections:

| December 8 | **GOOD ORDERLY DIRECTION** |

Yesterday, today, and tomorrow, I live and move in the one. Whatever I am feeling at any moment, I know that I am never alone. I bask in the inner glow of unfolding good. I remain steadfast in the inner glow, full of the love that I have allowed to flow. I remember who and what I am. As I take time to graciously accept my inner gifts as I have accepted my outer gifts, I say yes to each one unwrapping them gently, joyously, and with gratitude.

I receive. I accept. I embrace.

Reflections:

Yesterday, today, and tomorrow, I live and move in the one. Whatever I am feeling at any moment, I know that I am never alone. I feel discomfort within when I am impatient. Frustration and inconvenience will visit me, but I know that patience is the key. I am the spiritual warrior. The challenge of the spiritual warrior is always with the self. Patience is the key.

I receive. I accept. I embrace.

Reflections:

December 10   **GOOD ORDERLY DIRECTION**

Yesterday, today, and tomorrow, I live and move in the one. Whatever I am feeling at any moment, I know that I am never alone. As I reflect back over this year I know that very soon, I will be closing a chapter on this year. As I look at this year, I look at it with the understanding of my own Divinity. I look at it through the inner glow that I feel.

I receive. I accept. I embrace.

Reflections: _____
_____
_____
_____
_____

Ayin M. Adams, Ph.D. December 11

Yesterday, today, and tomorrow, I live and move in the one. Whatever I am feeling at any moment, I know that I am never alone. As I reflect back on this year, I see the people I have touched, and the people who have touched me. The experiences I have gone through whether they were happy or sad, or whatever I might have called them, as I was growing through them, today I look at them objectively. I am looking at the tapestry of my life with one stitch flowing into the other and seeing not individuals and separate experiences, but a picture, a picture that is the unfoldment that is me.

I receive. I accept. I embrace.

Reflections:

December 12   **GOOD ORDERLY DIRECTION**

Yesterday, today, and tomorrow, I live and move in the one. Whatever I am feeling at any moment, I know that I am never alone. No longer do I run or flee from my challenges. I know that as I continue to reflect back over this year, I see that some stitches on my tapestry have been a little bit blurred, some stitches very bright, and some stitches now that I look back at them, I can almost smile, because It has all been a part of my growth unfoldment. Finally, I can release this image. It is finished. It is all done.

I receive. I accept. I embrace.

Reflections: _____
_____
_____
_____
_____
_____

Yesterday, today, and tomorrow, I live and move in the one. Whatever I am feeling at any moment, I know that I am never alone. That experience which was beautiful was complete in itself. It has prepared me for something that is more beautiful. Those experiences which might have been sad, I know that through my spiritual understanding, they have been a part of my growth process. I can let go of them, so that the fruits may come from that too. And as I take time to begin the new chapter in the new me of the New Year, I am listening to hear within me that voice that is always saying, "Choose. Choose me this day."

I receive. I accept. I embrace.

Reflections: _____
_____
_____
_____
_____
_____

December 14   **GOOD ORDERLY DIRECTION**

LIFE'S TAPESTRY

Yesterday, today, and tomorrow, I live and move in the one. Whatever I am feeling at any moment, I know that I am never alone. No longer do I allow others to choose for me. I know that in the coming year, I will choose my own colors. I know the colors that I will weave and the patterns that I will allow to come forth on my tapestry. I refuse to let anyone choose for me. I know that my pattern is my uniqueness. I know that I will get so in tune with it, that I identify as It and relate to It so completely that It naturally flows through me.

I receive. I accept. I embrace.

Reflections:

Ayin M. Adams, Ph.D.　　　　　　December 15

Yesterday, today, and tomorrow, I live and move in the one. Whatever I am feeling at any moment, I know that I am never alone. I need not look at anyone else's colors. I know that their colors are right for them. Today, I know my colors. I know that every stitch is an outer evidence of a thought, a feeling, and an awareness that is me. I live my tapestry one day at a time with first things first. Today, I know how to let my life unfold, always out of that inner glow that is me, that inner flow that is me, and that inner glow that is awareness. I feel that inner glow right now.

I receive. I accept. I embrace.

Reflections: _____
_____
_____
_____
_____
_____

December 16   **GOOD ORDERLY DIRECTION**

Yesterday, today, and tomorrow, I live and move in the one. Whatever I am feeling at any moment, I know that I am never alone.

> Breath of Mother Earth
> Has nurtured me strong in love
> Through the winter's night

I receive. I accept. I embrace.

Reflections:

Yesterday, today, and tomorrow, I live and move in the one. Whatever I am feeling at any moment, I know that I am never alone. As I move into the sacredness of my own being, as I move into next year, I say "Yes!" everyday to the gift that is me. I choose…because I know who I am. I choose to become all that I am created to be. I know this is my gift. This is my freedom. This is my privilege. This is my responsibility, and out of this is my fulfillment. I am the inner glow that is the greatest celebration that man has ever known. Today, I can just be…graciously, joyously, with the anticipation of a little child, and the responsibility of spiritual maturity. I go forward and say "Yes!" So it is.

I receive. I accept. I embrace.

Reflections: _____
_____
_____
_____
_____
_____

December 18 — **GOOD ORDERLY DIRECTION**

LISTENING TO THE STILL SMALL VOICE

Yesterday, today, and tomorrow, I live and move in the one. Whatever I am feeling at any moment, I know that I am never alone. No longer do I listen to my own negative thinking. I know that there is guidance for me when I listen to the still small voice. I know that I will hear the right word.

I receive. I accept. I embrace.

Reflections:

Yesterday, today, and tomorrow, I live and move in the one. Whatever I am feeling at any moment, I know that I am never alone. I know that I must discipline myself to constantly heed the still small voice. I must listen to the Divine fountain within that is telling me the right and wise thing to do. I know that I am led into the fulfillment of the Divine Mind of everything that I have ever yearned for, everything that I need, and every challenge that faces me in my life. Today, I take time to be still and lowly listen, the process that is moving through me and expressing as me in the outworking of my own imprisoned splendor. I am setting myself free. Join me, friends.

I receive. I accept. I embrace.

Reflections:

December 20 **GOOD ORDERLY DIRECTION**

INSPIRATION

Yesterday, today, and tomorrow, I live and move in the one. Whatever I am feeling at any moment, I know that I am never alone. Within the depths of my being lies a deep desire to improve myself, which is really God inspiring me with a splendid idea. He who supplies me with that idea, and gives me the power to carry it out, is really God at the center of my being. I know that anytime I have a desire to grow or a hope or a yearning to be more, to do more, to have more, this is God tapping at the door of consciousness, leading me in the way of growth. I am God's inspiration.

I receive. I accept. I embrace.

Reflections:

Yesterday, today, and tomorrow, I live and move in the one. Whatever I am feeling at any moment, I know that I am never alone. There is a Divine Mind counterpart within me for all outward experiences. I sense this. I intuitively feel this. That is why I have a yearning, an aching to do something, because there is a Divine potential seeking to break loose from the shell of human consciousness and to express itself in fullness. I know that which I am seeking is already seeking me. I am God's inspiration.

I receive. I accept. I embrace.

Reflections:

December 22 — **GOOD ORDERLY DIRECTION**

REACTIONS

Yesterday, today, and tomorrow, I live and move in the one. Whatever I am feeling at any moment, I know that I am never alone. No longer do I look at my experiences as negative. I know that these are not negative experiences. They are negative reactions to experiences. I now make a commitment to be more positive and non-resistant.

I receive. I accept. I embrace.

Reflections: _____
_____
_____
_____
_____
_____

Yesterday, today, and tomorrow, I live and move in the one. Whatever I am feeling at any moment, I know that I am never alone. Negative reactions to experiences are emotions that I am feeling, that are burning up within me whether I am aware of it or not. These reactions have a great deal to do with my consciousness, my feelings, my faith, and my general well being. They indicate that I fall into a rut of self-limitation. I need to make a new commitment to finding the Divine level within myself always.

I receive. I accept. I embrace.

Reflections:

December 24 — **GOOD ORDERLY DIRECTION**

A WORKING CONSCIOUSNESS

Yesterday, today, and tomorrow, I live and move in the one. Whatever I am feeling at any moment, I know that I am never alone. I know that all things work together for good. I know that situations do not automatically get better. People say, "Well things will work out." Things will not work out, unless I work with them, unless I get in the consciousness in which they can work out. I have work to do to change my own consciousness.

I receive. I accept. I embrace.

Reflections: _____
_____
_____
_____
_____
_____

HOLIDAYS

Yesterday, today, and tomorrow, I live and move in the one. Whatever I am feeling at any moment, I know that I am never alone. I move into the true celebration of who I am. I know that Christmas, Hanukkah, and Kwanzaa are holidays. They are not just a day on a calendar, they are an experience. They are the light that is me. They are the love that is me. They are the life energy that would live as me. They are creativity, creating through me. I say, "Yes" to it.

I receive. I accept. I embrace.

Reflections:

December 26   **GOOD ORDERLY DIRECTION**

Yesterday, today, and tomorrow, I live and move in the one. Whatever I am feeling at any moment, I know that I am never alone. I know that Christmas has come and gone, now what? In the afterglow of Christmas I ask myself, "What is it that has come and gone? What is over until next year?" I know that if this experience, if this festival can be picked up and laid down, then it really has very little relevance to life. I must ask myself as a student of truth, as a student of life, what these statements and attitudes mean? I know that it is now time to prepare myself for entering into the New me, the New Year.

I receive. I accept. I embrace.

Reflections:

Yesterday, today, and tomorrow, I live and move in the one. Whatever I am feeling at any moment, I know that I am never alone. I must trust myself and ask for my desires to be met. Next I must believe that the desire is already mine. I know that it is on the way to demonstrate my unwavering faith. I must be open to receive that which I desired. I feel wonderful. I feel good, and I am happy.

I receive. I accept. I embrace.

Reflections:

December 28 **GOOD ORDERLY DIRECTION**

Yesterday, today, and tomorrow, I live and move in the one. Whatever I am feeling at any moment, I know that I am never alone. I claim all parts of myself that long to be held. I embrace my quiet strength that lives deep inside me. I am ready. I know that I am ready for that great change and I feel the shifting currents speaking to my soul.

I receive. I accept. I embrace.

Reflections:

WALKING IN NEW WAYS

Yesterday, today, and tomorrow, I live and move in the one. Whatever I am feeling at any moment, I know that I am never alone. No longer am I content to walk the old way. I know that the known way is the way of the past. It is the comfortable way. "Oh, I can do this work with my eyes closed." That is the known way. Walking the known way will make this coming year the same as every other year. In most cases I hear, "Well, same old thing! Nothing ever works for me." And nothing old will continue to work, as long as the walk is the known way. Be ready to walk in new ways.

I receive. I accept. I embrace.

Reflections:
_____
_____
_____
_____
_____
_____

December 30   **GOOD ORDERLY DIRECTION**

Yesterday, today, and tomorrow, I live and move in the one. Whatever I am feeling at any moment, I know that I am never alone. I am a spiritual being always and in all ways. I may not be aware of it, but it is my Divine potential. The fact is that I live in a physical body, and I live in a world of form and things. I know that sometimes I tend to lose this perspective and forget that life is lived from within out. I now know and remember that at any time, I can come to myself and arise and go to the father/mother/God/Goddess. I know that within me is this Divine potential that is always seeking release. I know that I can give birth to it at any time along life's' way.

I receive. I accept. I embrace.

Reflections:

AYIN'S BLESSING

Yesterday, today, and tomorrow, I live and move in the one. Whatever I am feeling at any moment, I know that I am never alone.

May the Lord God release me to fulfill the very purpose that he has called me to do. May I fulfill all the desires that God has for me. May I sense the longing and hunger of God for my own life. May I not be intimidated or threatened by anything or anyone. May I rise up and see my life coming into its full destiny. In the name of the Lord God, we give/ decree this blessing to you.

I receive. I accept. I embrace.

Reflections: _____
_____
_____
_____
_____
_____

TOPIC INDEX

A

A New Day .... August 1
A Working Consciousness .... December 24
Acceptance .... April 22, May 9, May 12
Accepting Self .... July 7
All Things Are Possible .... November 16
Answered Prayers .... May 23
Anxious .... March 23
Approval .... July 6
Ayin's Blessing .... December 31

B

Beloved .... July 26
Blessings .... February 15
Blockages .... July 23-24
Bringing Concerns to God .... February 26
Broader Spiritual Vision .... October 21

C

Call of the Soul .... March 16-17
Cautious Entanglements .... September 26
Change .... January 7, April 5, July 8
Choices .... March 1-6
Clarity .... April 14, June 13
Commitment .... July 30
Conditions .... July 2
Confidence .... October 1
Controlling Emotions .... March 12-13, March 25, November 5
Creative Waiting .... March 8, May 21-22, July 1

TOPIC INDEX

D

Death	April 26
Deep Commitment	June 30
Deep Desires	September 3
Difficulties	August 26
Direction for the Day	August 23
Discovering Depth	April 21, July 31, August 25
Disease	November 13
Divine Flow	June 5, August 22, November 3
Doorway to God	March 20
Dying In Order to Live	May 30

E

Ego (Easing God Out)	May 10
Embracing Clarity	February 9
Embracing Good	February 8
Embracing the Divinity of Self	November 26
Emotional Pain	March 22
Energy	June 26
Entering the Stillness	February 16-19

F

Faith	August 28, August 30
Faith Being Tested	March 21
Falling from Love	March 27
Fear	February 20-21
Feeding the Soul	August 31, September 27
Feelings	May 2, May 13
Focus	April 15-18

TOPIC INDEX

F, continued

Forgiveness	December 4-6
Forward Movement	July 21
Full Partnership	September 24

G

Gifts	December 17
Giving Up Old Ways	May 19
GOD	October 23-24
Going Within	May 6
Grace	September 20-23
Gratitude	November 6, November 9-12, November 17-22, November 27
Greater Freedom	July 17-18
Guidance	December 18

H

Harmony	September 10-12, December 3
Healing	April 30
Holidays	December 25
Honesty with Self	January 8
Honoring the Process	May 4
Hostages	December 1
Human Feelings	March 29
Humanitarian	November 24
Humility	July 22

I

Illuminating Spirit	April 28

TOPIC INDEX

I, continued

In the Silence	August 6, August 9
Inexhaustible Source	December 2
Infinite Life	January 6, July 4
Inner Glow	August 2, December 7-10
Inner Sanctuary	November 23
Inspiration	December 20
Intimacy	April 20, October 26-28
Inviting Spirit	July 14

J

Justice	January 16

K

Kindness	November 10
Kingdom	June 1

L

Lack	October 13
Let Go/Let Flow	July 15-16
Letting Go of the Past	January 12, January 14
Light	April 27
Limits	July 29
Living Between Worlds	March 15
Living in the Now	April 6
Loneliness	October 20
Loss	October 12
Love	January 25-29, May 16, June 19-21

TOPIC INDEX

L, continued

Loving Relationships .... January 31

M

Making Healthy Choices........................ March 9
Making Love.. February 22
Making Peace with the Past .... March 26
Metamorphosis....................................... January 10
Minding My Own Business .... October 2-3
Mother.. August 4
Movement .... April 10

N

Networking with Heaven .... February 23
Never No in Infinite Mind..................... April 4
New Beginnings Follow Change .... February 27
New Chapter/New Year .... January 1-2, December 13
New Day/New Beginning..................... September 9
No Separation.. February 11, August 14
Now Moment .... April 8

O

Only Me .... September 4
Outgrowing Form.................................. September 19
Overly Involved .... May 3

P

Pain .... April 25, September 30
Patience .... April 12-13, May 18,
                                                      February 29, December 9

TOPIC INDEX

P, continued

Perseverance	May 17, November 30
Personal Inventory	January 3, January 5
Pool of Reserve	June 14
Prayer	February 6, February 12-14, June 15-17, August 10-12
Pressure	August 15-17
Pride and Presumption	May 15
Problems	March 31, June 18
Prosperity	October 4-11

Q

Quiet Strength	December 28

R

Reactions	December 22-23
Realization	August 18, August 20
Ready	March 10
Regeneration	June 25
Relationships:	
Authentic	January 23
Being the Right Person	January 18
Forming	January 17
Frankness and Honesty	January 24
Expectations	January 19-20
Unreal Expectations	January 21
Relaxation	September 16-18
Resentments	January 13
Responsibility	September 13

TOPIC INDEX

S

Sadness	June 11-12
Searching for Peace	September 8, November 25
Seeing Beyond Appearances	April 1
Self Love	January 30, February 1-2, May 7, May 11
Selflessness	November 29
Serenity	September 8
Spiritual Armor Prayer	February 24-25
Spiritual Bank Account	September 28
Spiritual Being	December 30
Spiritual Blueprint	July 11
Spiritual CPR	October 30
Spiritual Discernment	September 29
Spiritual Freedom	February 4-5
Spiritual Love	June 20-21
Standstill	March 19
Storm	April 19
Suffering	February 28
Surrender	April 7
Synchronized with the Universe	February 7

T

Taking Healthy Action	September 25
Taking Power Back	May 5
Tapestry of Life	December 11-12, December 14-15
Time	January 4
Transparency	March 14
Trust	May 14

T, continued

Trust Account	August 29
Trusting Test	October 29
Trusting the Process	April 9

U

Unhappen Things	January 11
Universal Energy	February 10

V

Victory	Unknown

W

Wait Upon the Will of Heaven	December 23
Waiting is an Occupation	May 24
Walking in New Ways	February 3, December 29
Walking with God	March 24
Willingness to Give	July 28
Winter of Life	October 31
Wisdom	July 27
Witness	July 9-10
Wholeness	July 25

Y

Yes	January 30, April 3, September 5-6

About the Author

Ayin M. Adams, PhD, Msc.D, is a native New Yorker. She is also an international metaphysician, spiritual director, and intuitive therapist. Adams is a holistic teacher of self-development and consciousness. Adams utilizes her gift of words to heal, educate, and entertain.

Adams is the author of more than seven books. Adams has been published by *"Women in the Moon"* publishing, *Bum Rush, The Page, In The Family*, and *Quiet Mountain Essays*. Adams is the winner of numerous awards and grants, including the 1998 *Pat Parker Poetry Award*, the 1999 *Audre Lorde Memorial Prose Prize*, the 2001 *President's Award for Literary Excellence*, and the *Zora Neal Hurston/Richard Wright Award*. Adams documents our passage in time using her writings and tonality of voice to help one break out of the current constraints and fragmentation of daily and habitual life. She assists and facilitates individuals to co-create their futures, especially as many of the established structures of society may be falling apart. Adams lives with the intention of suiting up, showing up, and following through. Adams embraces a firm belief that everything is in Divine Order. Ayin M. Adams organizes and leads spiritual retreats geared towards the transformational transcendence of mind, body, and soul. You may visit her at www.ayinadams.com.

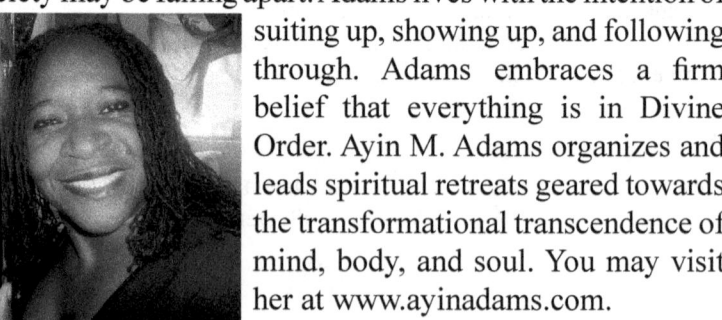

www.ingramcontent.com/pod-product-compliance
Lightning Source LLC
Chambersburg PA
CBHW070715160426
43192CB00009B/1202